Surfcasting

BLOCK ISLAND
AND CUTTYHUNK

Surfcasting
BLOCK ISLAND
AND CUTTYHUNK

D. J. MULLER

BURFORD BOOKS

Printed in the United States of America.

10 9 8 7 6 5 4 3 2 1

Library of Congress Cataloging-in-Publication Data
is on file with the Library of Congress

Contents

Acknowledgments

The writing of a book is a lot of work (I always say that). Lots of writing, editing, collecting good photos, it feels really good when it comes time to hit the send button and send the final package off to the publisher! I would like to dedicate this book to "my loves," my wife Jenn and daughter Keilana. Two amazing people for sure and I really appreciate them and their patience with me being in "my hole." I also dedicate it to my other love, my wonderful daughter Hillary whom I love deeply and am very proud of!

Of course also to all my buds that were around, and are always around, as I wrote this labor of love: Murty, Frank Giacolone, Jolliffe, Joe C., Beth Bushell, Lellis. Plus the other 50 that help make life great!

I dedicate it to my very, very good friend, Ronnie Bala who went home to fish the big surf on January 23, 2019. Ronnie helped enrich hundreds—no, thousands—of surfcasters' experiences by getting good products into their hands. He was always willing to help and he was loved by many! Godspeed my friend!!

As I have done numerous times in the past, I also acknowledge my chiropractor Dr. Barbara Costa (Sea Coast Family

Chiropractic, Pt. Pleasant Beach, NJ) as she has be keeping me "straight" and healthy for a very long time. She is very good at what she does. Surfcasting can be extremely tough on you physically—as an example, I remember the time when I did a face plant on Block one night and jammed my neck. She got me fixed up back to feeling good. Thank you for giving me a good quality of life!

I also want to acknowledge Bonnie "Darling Hat" Veeder for all her love and help throughout the years and all that she has done to preserve the Cuttyhunk Fishing Club in its present state. It is my sincere wish that the club stands forever, for its historical importance to our sport of surfcasting roots is irreplaceable. And for all the good times and happiness it continues to bring fishermen today in much the same way it did for our predecessors over a hundred and fifty years ago!

I would like to say thank you to John Paul (JP) Hunter the captain and owner of the "Cuttyhunk Water Taxi," most commonly known as *The Seahorse* for just being a good dude! He is a sheer pleasure. One of the kindest, sweetest guys that you will ever meet and he has been there since my early days.

In the writing of the history of Cuttyhunk, I was inundated with numerous sources and accounts of what happened there over the years, as you might figure dates and stories and renditions overlapped or conflicted. I wrote what I determined was the best version of what really happened, and since it is all in the past now we may never know for sure. I reported the information I gathered objectively and I submitted it with great respect and neutrality.

In the chapter on Cuttyhunk history I need to thank the following people for their help or for providing a resource:

Kathryn Ellen Bulter from the Museum of the Elizabeth Islands and the Cuttyhunk Historical Society. The Cuttyhunk Historical Society for publishing great articles and literature on Cuttyhunk and Pasque Islands. Margaret Brewer's, "Cuttyhunk As I Remember It." The Cuttyhunk Historical Society, Monograph, Summer 2013, "The Era of the Fishing Club: Fishing with Gilded Hook," by Kathyrn Balistrieri. Also "Cuttyhunk and the Elizabeth Islands from 1602," published by the Cuttyhunk Historical Society, 1993. All incredible and valuable resources!

I also need to thank the staff of the Block Island Historical Society, who were helpful when we did a tour of the museum. It was very informative and I see the Museum as a very important and necessary part of Block Island's rich past. It really helped me understand the culture of Block Island's development.

I need to acknowledge John Swienton and his tackle shop and apartments at the Twin Maples on Block Island. He has for a long time been a friend to me and other surfcasters that have come and stayed at the Twin Maples, and he has always gone out of his way to help put us onto fish. Even if you didn't stay there he is always willing to help with a map, information, and perhaps get you some live eels for lunker hunting.

Also Gary Soldati and his crew Rod and Ted for showing me the ropes of Block Island many years ago.

Lastly my Lord Jesus Christ from whom all good things come. "Some go to church and think about fishing, others go fishing and think about God!" That's me!

"It's better to go fishing with your kid today than to go hunting for him tomorrow."—Author unknown

Preface

Well she is done, I have completed my fifth book. When I was in college if you told me I would end up writing five books on surfcasting I would have said, "I will write five books on what??" Although I have always written on various subjects (non-school related), even before high school, if you told me that I would end up writing about fishing I probably would have scratched my head as well as laughed out loud and (unfortunately) in your face. Even though I have been fishing since a was a young punk boy.

The question I ask myself is—why do I do it? I thought hard about the question. Monetarily, writing books is a dud. Al Ristori, whom I consider a good friend, told me you will never make money writing a book, it has to be "a labor of love." I have found his words to ring true over and over, but still here I am. I believe that I write because I love sharing my passion, I enjoy teaching and watching guys blossom into respectable surfcasters, and I want others to appreciate all the fascinating and fulfilling experiences that surfcasting has brought me throughout my surfcasting career. The places I have traveled, the characters I have fished with, the history of many of these places will stay with me forever and it has only deepened my appreciation of the whole. I can only hope that my work and industry can be carried on in others both now and long after I am gone. For those that have come and gone before me and for those that will follow, we will all have walked the same shorelines and scanned the same water and found good fishing, then we will be gone, yet the passion, much like the fish we pursue, will always remain the same.

Now a few things about this latest project: on the Around the Island chapters I didn't want to inundate the book with photos of boulderfields, because once you see one boulderfield, you have seen them all. I included a couple to give you an idea of what to expect, but you will have to do a good amount of scouting upon your arrival to either one of these great destinations. The Around the Island chapters are about details of the different spots.

When it came to equipment I did only a few photos of lures with the premise that if you are going out to fish these islands, you probably already have a good idea of what the various lures are and what they look like.

When it came to writing about the history of Block Island, there was very little that was clear, so I resorted to S.T. Livermore's, *History of Block Island* (a great read), originally written in 1877 and re-published by the Block Island Historical Society numerous times. That was enough credibility for me. I appreciated Livermore's accounts, his looking back as well as his memories from talking to old people from when he was young and gathering his stories in a grassroots process. As far as I could see, he covered a lot of years that way, almost first-hand as well as gathering great and credible information from his own experiences.

Native Americans on Block started as the Manisses Indians, part of the greater Narraganset Tribe. At some point still unclear to me the Indians of Block split into two different tribes—the east side were the Narragansett and the west side became Pequot. I guess I get that, but in my studies I could not figure out when or why they became the Niantics, which they have been referred to several times in different places. Since I couldn't find anything substantial or concrete in my research I left that entire bit of information out. I point you back to Livermore's accounts.

Maps

My maps are very basic and done for reference. Cuttyhunk is fairly easy, but Block Island has a thousand spots with names, much different from Cuttyhunk.

The map of Cuttyhunk has a lot of names that my crew and I have come up with over the years. If there were official names I would use them of course, but I hunted high and low for names and came up with very little. I remember the day I was out with the great Cuttyhunk boat captain, Jimmy Nunes on the *Rudy-J* and he was rattling off the spots, but in no way could I ever remember any of them. The only three "official" names I have listed are these: Bass Bend, Barges Beach and Churches.

For Block Island I again just gave reference locations as there are many, many names used on the island. I suggest upon your arrival on Block Island that you go to the Star Department Store (directly across from the ferry) and buy one of their detailed maps, also go to Twin Maples (on Beach Road) and grab one of their maps, get a report and maybe buy a couple things to support the islanders.

I woke and dragged myself out of bed. I stumbled down the hall like a zombie and turned left into the kitchen. Lellis was standing there staring at the coffee pot with this blank look on his face. Jolliffe was sitting with his legs crossed, looking out the window. I gave half an effort as I asked Lell how he did last night. Without moving his head and in a monotone voice he mumbled, "Last night I caught the biggest fish that I have ever seen." I said "Oh." I turned and walked away when suddenly I stopped short and turned around and I said, "What did you say?" He repeated the sentence. I woke up. I want to share his story with you.

Lellis arrived at our spot just as we were heading back to the Clubhouse. He had been doing well on the top end of the tide while Mark and I had been fishing the bottom half of the tide on the incoming. I got off my rock and Lellis got on it. Lellis relayed to me, as I sipped hot coffee, that he picked away at fish starting about a half hour after we left. He was going to fish until 1 a.m. and then get back because we were hitting the road for home early the next morning. He said he picked good fish the entire time up to 18 lbs. One o'clock came and it was time to go, but he had a couple of more good hook-ups and then said screw it, 2 a.m. cut-off. He fished on. He had 18 fish and decided he was going to go for 20 then head back. Suddenly he hooked into a big fish, which he thought for most of the time was a foul-hooked 25-pounder. The fish made three long, powerful runs. It would pull out a load of drag and he would reel it back in only to have the fish do another long run straight out. On the last run the fish went off to the left and into the boulders where he thought he was going to break it off. He let off the fish (gave it slack), hoping the fish would run back out, straight out, which it did with another long run. At this point the fish turned and swam directly towards him. He thought that he had lost the fish as the line went slack, but upon catching up to contact he realized that the fish was still there. Almost ten minutes in he finally got the fish close, and the big fish was tired (so was he). At this point he thought he only wants to see this fish, and he wanted to be sure he didn't kill it. When he turned on his light, through heavy fog and wet glasses he was surprised to see another fish, which he thought was a shark, right behind his fish. A shark? He was shocked when he realized that it wasn't another fish at all, rather it was the fish's tail!

The fish was massive! He got the fish on a 2-ounce Hab needle. The needle was stuck on the inside of the fish's jaw. The treble was in the jaw, one of the hooks was broken off, the single Siwash tailhook hung free. After removing the lure he reached down and grabbed the fish by the bottom lip with two hands. Both fists were across the lip with an inch and a half space between the fists. He lifted the fish up as high as he could to his chest. He was ankle-deep on his rock, and the fish's tail was still 12" in the water. (I watched as he showed me where he had lifted the fish to, he's 6'5", it was equal to my Sphenoid process, or the very top of my rib cage.) I measured from there to the floor, it was 48-inches, add another 12 and shit!! That's 60 inches! He said his absolute concern was keeping the fish alive. He (of course) didn't have a camera with him but he wanted to get an idea of the fish's length so he laid the fish and the rod down beside each other on his rock. While trying to organize the two a wave came in and knocked him down and he lost his rod. He scrambled to recover his rod and went back to find the fish, but the fish was gone. He scanned the nearby rocks for the washed up beast but it was nowhere to be found. That was good for him knowing the great fish swam away. We estimated the fish to be a least mid-60's.

It is for this reason that I pursue the islands.

My friend and fellow island-hopper Tom Kosinski sent me this photo with the mere caption, "A hundred crappy nights." This fish weighed forty-eight and a half pounds, a beautiful fish by any standard. As surfcasters we fish long and we fish hard in pursuit of a fish like this and a fish like this doesn't come within range very often. So when it does and you fool it, it is extremely satisfying! Releasing it only makes the catch that much sweeter.

CHAPTER ONE

Introduction to the Islands of Block and Cuttyhunk

There is something about going to an island to fish. The tranquility, the beautiful sunsets, the lack of pressure simply due to the effort it takes to get to an island in the first place. Experiencing the culture, learning the history, meeting local people—it all adds substance to the experience, one I find compelling and challenging.

The wild and unpredictable striped bass lives its life in search of food. As a surfcaster you search for places where bass come and stay for a while, holding and feeding daily, as opposed to a place where the fish are migrating and constantly on the move. You have to "hit 'em where they live," I like to say.

There are places all along our coast where bass migrate to in the spring, spending some time there before they head south once again in the fall. Two such places are Block Island and Cuttyhunk Island. Both are places I have fished extensively and have gotten to know very well in my travels. I wrote this book because I felt that a resource on fishing these two gems would be helpful for the surfcaster looking to enter a new world of striper fishing.

As an introduction to the islands, and in an effort to not be redundant, I am going to cover the similarities of the two islands here, as they do have much in common. I will then be much more specific when I address each island independently in the chapters that follow.

GEOLOGY

Thousands of years ago a huge glacier moved across the land, pushing and plowing as it moved. When the glacier melted away it left some great striper terrain. The "Outer Lands" was a moraine responsible for forming much our great striper grounds, including Block Island and Cuttyhunk Island, and is responsible for the rolling hills and boulder-strewn coastlines on both islands. It reached down through Massachusetts,

The great Outer Lands Moraine, a massive glacier, moved through New England giving us some of the best striper terrain in the world, with boulderfields scattered all along the northeast coast. Block Island and Cuttyhunk Island both offer considerable boulderfields for surfcasters to fish.

Rhode Island, and New York, forming the peninsula of Cape Cod and the islands of Martha's Vineyard, the Elizabeth Islands, Nantucket, Block Island, and Long Island, as well as surrounding islands and islets.

Even though the majority of these islands are rock, the island shoreline structure changes from year to year, mostly due to intense winter storms with large waves that batter these unprotected coastlines.

WEED RING

Before I first arrived on Cuttyhunk I was told in no uncertain terms that the island had a weed ring around it, and it was true. Not just one weed either, but a mix of weeds. Block Island also has a weed ring, and not just seaweed—sometimes you will run into mung, the curse of the surfcaster. Mung is a fine red weed that once it hits your line it will stick. It makes a mess and is very tough to pick off your line and clips. If there is any kind of weed on your line, or lure, a fish won't even look at it. Many fishermen get deterred by the weed. They look in the water and see it, say the water is dirty, and then leave. But what they don't realize is that the weed only extends out sometimes only ten feet or sometimes ten to 15 yards—beyond that the water is as clear as gin. I didn't fully realize this until I started wetsuiting, which allowed me to push out a lot further than I could have done in waders. The lesson is simple: Do not be fooled or deterred when you see the weed.

It was late June when a storm pushed in over Block from Montauk, your typical fast-moving afternoon thunderstorm. We were staying at the Twin Maples and John told us that usually after a front pushes through, that west side lights up pretty good. So we geared up and shot over to Grace's as the turbid weather calmed down and we all went out and got a rock and started casting. The entire area was loaded with eel grass and there were only patches here and there where there was no grass. Any time you hit one of those weedless patches with the pencil, worked it for a few seconds, you had a fish on. It was amazing and weird but we had a great hit into the dark. As a surfcaster I had learned that weed had little impact on what the fish wanted. It was up to me to work with, or around, the weed.

It wouldn't be fair if I didn't mention bubbleweed. My very good friend Tommy Bozan was sure to emphasize to me that it was officially kelp. My other buddy Bill Lellis tells me that its official name is "rockweed" or "Maine rockweed" and it is kelp. So while it may be kelp and it may be rockweed, to me it will always be bubbleweed. Bubbleweed thrives in the boulderfields and both islands have plenty of it! It is a very long, rigid weed that has little pockets of bubble-like pods on them. Bubbleweed is an intricate part of the shallows—at low tide it lays on the rocks and at high tide it floats. If you walk on the slippery weed and rocks at low tide it can easily put you on your can, cleats or no cleats. It grows to up to five feet long. For me the bubbleweed is the indicator of how deep water is, if I see the weed I know I am in relatively shallow water or water three to five feet deep. If I am in an unfamiliar area at night and I find a nice rock, once I get up on it, I will light up the area out in front of me, and if I see a lot of bubbleweed in the boulders, I move on. If all I see is water I know I have deep water in front of me. The last thing you want to do is reel a lure, or worse a bass, through bubbleweed.

Bubbleweed is also handy for grabbing onto and pulling yourself up on to that big rock that you are trying to get on.

PREVAILING WIND

The prevailing wind on these two islands is southwest. The southwest wind at either one of these places won't hurt you, it will only help.

One of the problems with fishing an island is that a really hard, sustained wind from any direction can "blow out" the entire island as the wind sweeps fast down both sides of the shoreline, dirtying the water as it churns. I've been stuck on Block with 60 mile-an-hour winds, the ferry shut down so we aren't going anywhere and nowhere to fish. Now that really hurts!

WATER MOVEMENT AND MOON PHASE

One of my favorite things about fishing these islands are the better-than-average water movements that run along them. I love sweep, as do the striped bass, the faster the water moves the better they feed and of course when they are on the feed, you catch! I grew up fishing the sandy beaches of New Jersey where pull or sweep is almost non-existent. They say normal beaches pull at a half a knot. If I had to make an educated guess I would say that the islands pull at around two to three knots, compared to the Cape Cod Canal that pulls at four to six knots, possibly more. Water speeds are also impacted by wind speed and wind direction, as well as moon phase.

Let's talk a little bit about moon phase as this is a big factor. On the new and full moons, the moon comes closest to the earth. The gravitation pull of the moon wants to pull the water off the earth, which causes extra high and extra low tides. For a couple of days the tides are usually a foot or two (sometimes more) higher than on a normal quarter-moon tide when the gravitational pull is much less. A tide cycle still has to take 6 hours and 15 minutes, so you have to figure that with the extra water of a moon tide, that extra volume of a foot or two, the water still has to move within the 6 hour, 15 minute confine, so the water has to move a lot faster than normal to make up for the extra volume. Increased water speed leads to increased production a lot of the time.

Now let's talk about the guy that says he likes to fish the downside of the new moon, meaning the few days following a new or full moon. Why do you think this is a good time? Because of barometric pressure, or that the fish are like werewolves and get hungrier and suicidal on a full or new moon? No. What I believe happens is that the fish use the strong moon tides to travel long distances, to transport themselves quickly, from Point A to Point B, with minimal effort. So what happens is on the moons new bodies of fish arrive into certain areas. So where there were no fish last week, suddenly this week there are fish! That said, it can also move fish out of an area. I have had that happen too, ruining a good hit.

So let's now talk about the islands. For three years in a row I fished Cuttyhunk on the new moon of October, the Hunter's

Moon. That was when I was told it was a great time to be there and boy was I ready to catch Moby Dick the striper. For those three years I struggled to have good weeks, they were downright slow. I was frustrated so I put some thought into it. What I came up with was that during the big moons, the water pulls very fast along the island so the bass, instead of coming into the shallows to feed at night, were more inclined to sit in the depressions just off the coast and let the "conveyor belt" feed them—less effort, more reward. I put my theory to the test the next season, when instead of fishing the big moon, I fished the quarter moon, my premise being that when the water moved slower the bass (hopefully larger ones) were more inclined to come into the shallows to feed on lobster, crabs, blackfish, and cunner, because they didn't have to fight the big currents. The results: 100+ fish with an occasional heavyweight. Need I say more?

WETSUITING

You certainly don't need a wetsuit to fish Block Island or Cuttyhunk, however, if you are serious about fishing it and delving deep into the hunt for good bass, I strongly recommend you wear one if you don't already. For many, "wetsuiting" is associated with swimming out through deep dark waters, fighting strong currents and beasts of the night. It doesn't have to be so dramatic. The wearing of the wetsuit is not about swimming three miles out to a rock or doing anything crazy, but it is about access and freedom from worry, and about safety. Waders can be a pain, they can rip easily when walking through or around barnacle-encrusted rocks, and once they leak, you're done. Walking around with water in your boots is a terrible feeling and is downright work! Wear a wetsuit and you can walk freely anywhere you want to go. Get down on your knees, lie down, get up, no worries. Your legs and arms are protected from bugs, sticker bushes, poison ivy, and cuts from sharp objects. Trust me, the wetsuit will free your mind from worry and allow you to concentrate more on fishing. There was an older gentleman who came up to me at one of the shows, long white beard, and he was looking for confirmation that a wetsuit was a good idea, even for him. He must have been in his early 70s and he was in great shape. So I gave him my spiel on why wetsuiting was a good idea regardless of age and that swimming was in no way necessary to be effective. Well he bought in! Every year, I think it's been five years now, he has come back telling me great stories and thanking me for opening his eyes.

When you fish places like Montauk, Block Island, Squibnocket, and Cuttyhunk, places with large sprawling boulderfields, the best way to attack them is by pushing out past what I call "the reef" or the shallow-water boulder and grass areas and get out to the edge where the water begins to get deep—this is where the fish will often congregate. Sometimes you will walk out 30 or 40 yards, sometimes 50 or 60 yards! Normally I get out to where I am waist- to chest-deep, where the water is beginning to get deep, maybe three to five feet deep. Once I am there I get up on a nice comfortable (flat) rock and begin fishing. I am now casting to deep water, five to ten feet deep normally. Doing this in waders is tough and daunting, doing this in a wetsuit is a piece of cake.

Although not essential, the wetsuit allows access that would never be attained in waders. Finding a good platform to fish from makes a big difference.

Now all this said about wetsuits, you still need to be in decent physical shape, especially if you are going to really push out or swim. If you are going to stay closer to shore then it is not as important. You don't really want to come to the islands without doing some kind of physical conditioning, as it will definitely diminish your enjoyment level.

Wetsuit Thickness

In the summer when water temperatures are 64–70 degrees, a 3-millimeter wetsuit will be fine. Spring and fall, with water temps in the high 50s to low 60s, a 4-mil will work although you may want to go up to a 5-mil if you will be dealing with long periods on the rocks or heavy winds. Regardless of time of the year I always carry an extra dive vest, just in case. The one I use is a 2.5-mil vest that zips up in front. This will add 2.5 mil to your core and should provide enough added warmth in most conditions.

IMPORTANT ADVISORY ON WETSUITING

Now I mention the wetsuit with a lot of emphasis and passion because I know how it has changed my fishing in terms of access to good water. But I need to say this: if you haven't wetsuited before, neither one of these islands would be a good place to start because of the remoteness of some of the locations—areas where there will be no help should something go wrong. You should cut your teeth on your home waters. And even an experienced person should *never* wetsuit alone in remote areas. There are places on both islands where you could scream until you are blue in the face and you will never be heard.

The other point I want to pound home is just because you have a wetsuit doesn't mean you have to swim anywhere. Ninety percent of the time I wade out and crawl up on a boulder. *Swimming in a wetsuit needs to be learned and practiced with someone who has plenty of experience.* The currents on these islands pull very hard—keep that in mind and always think safety first.

Waves and Swell

For those of you that are thinking about wetsuiting for the first time I would recommend going slow and building confidence in the seal costume. Eventually you will push out to the edge and you may have to deal with wave action or swell. This will be an adjustment period. I am going to begin by telling you that it is terribly important for you to stand and study the water and the rock you are considering—I sometimes watch for five to ten minutes. When looking for a rock out in water that has wave action or swell, my goal is to find a rock where the water doesn't roll over the rock higher than my thighs. I am searching for roughly two feet of water above the top of the rock, as a wave or swell rolls across it. Water hitting you waist-high or higher will quickly deter you as you will get

Getting out past the reef and the weed line and fishing the edge is pivotal on the islands. If you can get out to where the swell is, you will be better off than where waves can smack you.

knocked off your rock with regularity. Tide may come into my consideration as well, if the tide is dropping I may go for a marginal rock. If it's on the flood I will look elsewhere, as the water will only get deeper.

If you are going to be more aggressive with the wetsuit, you will need to be ready to take a beating. There are times, usually in rougher surf when a hard wind is pushing the water, where you will have to work hard to get to your rock. Once you get on you may have to strategize how to stay on it. For me I want to be out far enough to where I am in the swell and not getting hit by breaking waves. Swell is easier to deal with than waves smacking you. The determination of staying on a rock, or getting back onto a rock after being knocked off, will be directly associated with how good the fishing is. I have had nights when I have gotten knocked off 20 to 30 times but I would get right back up because the fishing was solid. Believe me, getting knocked off of your rock in darkness, getting carried toward the beach and then trying to find your rock again, can wear you down. I also want to mention positioning on the rock. My objective is to minimize the surface area of a wave hit, and I do this by keeping my legs spread apart. The second thing is at times you need to stand with your body braced against the hit. This will be a definite learning curve for the rookies. I keep my legs spread to about shoulder width and I keep one leg slightly forward and the other slightly back, never side-by-side. This way water can push through the "wickets" with little resistance, and you still have leverage when needed to withstand the momentary push of the water. Always keep your knees slightly bent as well—the last thing you want is hyperextension of the knee because a wave smacked unexpectedly Sometimes they catch you off guard.

Wading the Boulderfields

The wetsuit allows you to wade out past the rocks and bubbleweed safely. The rod works as a wading staff, a much-needed third leg. You could never do this in waders—too much chance of cutting your waders on sharp objects.

Wading the boulderfields is a must when wetsuiting and when fishing both of these islands, it is something that you will have to learn and eventually love to do. When wading out ten yards or 50 yards, usually through shallow water filled with bubbleweed/kelp, you will have a very difficult time doing it with just your two feet. Some use a wading staff, I just use my rod to help me with balance and stability, a third leg. The problem I had with that was I ended up hooking my finger around my collecting guide to keep it from sliding, and eventually it came loose from my hanging onto it, and that is not a good thing. I then proceeded to develop what I call "a wading grip" which was basically a grip to keep your wet hand from sliding down the rod while wading. It worked like a charm and I have put them on all the rods I use for wading. If you are going to use your rod as a wading staff you will need to be sure that your reel is submersible. Van Staal and ZeeBaaS reels would be examples.

This is the grip I came up with to keep your wet hand from sliding down the rod constantly while wading. I named it simply, The Wading Grip. It is an underwrap of cork, four or five O-rings, topped with Japanese shrink tubing. No more hanging on to the collecting guide.

AGENDA FISHING

I always come up with very specific plans or an agenda for my nightly fishing sessions. While I am scouting I am looking for a specific spot that jumps out at me or piques my interest. That spot goes into my "possibility file." After I do all of my scouting, and remember scouting is a *very* big part of this type of fishery, I then prioritize my spots. Some are made a priority by tidal stage, some by wind direction, some by intuition or gut feeling. On Block, it is much easier to move from one spot to the next because you can drive just about anywhere fairly quickly. On Cuttyhunk you have to be a little more deliberate and dedicated to a spot. On Cuttyhunk a move means some valuable time and effort since you have to walk just about everywhere you want to go. One of the things that I like about fishing these islands is that I have multiple options for the night. When I fish, of course I am looking for good fish, big fish, but I also love experimenting and fishing and figuring things out, fishing based on common sense and logic. "This spot looks very good because there is a nice drop-off here and I think on the outgoing when the water is moving left to right, and the wind is blowing southeast hard, there should be fish stacked up here." This is the kind of thought process that you need to come up with when fishing an ever-changing island. Good planning and very little guessing is the best way to target fish.

BLUFFS

Both of these beautiful islands have bluffs, high towering cliffs that overlook the sea. The bluffs come into play on both islands. One issue I have dealt with several times is when serious thunder storms were able to sneak up over on top of me that I never saw coming because of the bluffs, suddenly appearing with powerful lightning and forcing me to run for cover. As you know there isn't much cover on an open beach.

The bluffs also factor in when heavy rains bombard the island. When the heavy rains come the water washes down the face of the bluffs running through the silt and clay. If the rain falls hard and is sustained, the muddy water ends up in the ocean and can dirty the inshore water and ruin the fishing in that area. This is very important to keep in mind when weather is a factor. If you have dirty water on Block you may have to hunt hard for clean water. The west side is

Both islands have high bluffs consisting of clay and aggregates that fall into the sea when heavy rains or big seas roll in. The points and coves make for some great striper terrain.

a good option, because usually the west side is less affected by rain water. As often as possible, check the water you plan on fishing before dark to make sure it's clean, especially after some rain or real hard wind!

The bluffs are also eroding constantly and dare I say quickly. Every year when I go to either of these islands I am surprised to see how extensively the bluffs change by the combination of hard rain, sea-erosion, and coastal storms. One example would be the bluff that overlooks the Pyramids at Cuttyhunk. The Pyramids themselves where once the four concrete bases for a radar tower during World War II, that sat high upon the bluff. When I started fishing Cuttyhunk they were tight to the bottom of the bluffs, still a decent distance from the water. Now those mighty bluffs are gone and the Pyramids are beginning to sit in the water.

Another issue I see is that the erosion is also leading to shallower water and shoaling taking place in certain areas around the island. The rock and sand and clay all have to go somewhere. So I think at times the erosion of the bluffs leads to shallower water, which is exactly what we don't really want as surfcasters. How do we beat this? Simple: scout, push out further, and find your deep water.

FOG

You can't ever underestimate fog when you are on the islands. High levels of moisture in the air are common, especially at night. When the land warms during the day, especially in the summer, colliding with cool night air coming off the cooler water, fog will happen. Sometimes it moves in quick and can catch you off guard. One summer night on Cuttyhunk, my good friend Mark Jolliffe and I were fishing away when a pea-soup-thick fog rolled in on us. When you turn your light on you are instantly blinded, complete white-out, it can be a little freaky. This particular night there was zero wind and absolutely no surf, it was dead calm. I loaded up on a cast and let it go. Mark was about 100 yards away from me and he yelled out of the fog, "What are you doing?" I said "Fishing you big dummy!" Then he said, "I just heard what sounded like a lure land behind me!" I did a quick assessment and then realized that what I thought was straight out was really facing him, off to my left at about 10 o'clock. It was so weird! In the fog I lost my sense of direction, almost like vertigo. Now when coming off the rock, you are sometimes out 50–60 yards and you need to find your way back, but you can't see. Usually you can listen to hear the surf breaking then you know which way to go. On this particular night there was no surf, no wind, no visibility, so the only way to find your way back was by getting in the water and walking. If it got deeper you knew you were going the wrong way, turn around. It's hilarious—once you find the shoreline that is!

LIGHTNING

Previously I mentioned lightning and its impact on the islands. Before I head out nightly I always check my weather app to see what may be in store, then plan accordingly. The last thing you want to do is get caught in a nasty lightning storm, it could be deadly and more than once while out on the islands I almost got nailed. I remember three times I felt my rod buzzing and vibrating, which means you are about to get struck. I was out in the water and didn't know what to do so I just stuck my lightning rod under the water. Hell why not? Another time several of us got caught out at Sandy Point. There was a nasty, nasty storm that night, hail and high winds, so intense we threw our rods away and hunkered down on a log, in a depression on the beach and prayed to God for mercy. I thought for sure we were going to die, and to this day I am surprised we didn't.

The problem is that at times, especially on Block, you can watch big storms out over Long Island and they will stay there for hours, even though from a distance it looks like Armageddon is taking place. So you keep fishing. Once one of those storms lets go, and comes towards you, you run for the truck! You never know out there, I have watched many storms go around Block or Cuttyhunk, off to the north or south, and the weather on the island is never affected. So you can't stop fishing just because you see stuff many miles away, but you do have to be extremely careful and vigilant. Remember most of the time these storms are fast moving, they will come and they will blow right over and be done in an hour or so and you get right back to fishing. On other nights you may call it an early night because you see the weather map is all yellows and reds, so you go out socializing and good-timing.

DISAPPEARING BOULDERS

I noticed on both islands that one year I would go out on a point and have a rock that I would swear the good Lord sent me from heaven. You know—big, flat, with easy access. The next season I would go back to find it and it would be gone. One year I had a rock on Block that was to die for and I did really well on it. I went back to the same place the next year . . . no rock, nothing. But it was the size of a Volkswagen Mini-bus!

How can this happen? Ask any of the guys that spend a lot of time on rocks, and they'll tell you that the water in front of the rock is always a lot deeper than the water behind the rock. I believe this happens when the powerful waves blast into those rocks and force water over them, while at the same time blasting water straight down, etching a hole in front of the rock. It would not be uncommon to have four feet of water behind the rock and six feet or more in front. Sooner or later the rock falls into its own hole, and it's goodbye old friend!

The water in front of some of the huge boulders can be ridiculously deep. A buddy of mine Matt, who we call Dilly Dock, tried to get on one of those huge boulders down towards the West End of Cuttyhunk one day. Sometimes in order to get on some of the big boulders you have to swim around to the front and have a wave wash you up onto the boulder (hopefully not over it). So he was trying to get up on this beautiful plat-form and he was having some difficulty, working really hard without a lot of success. He said at one point, while in front of the rock and treading water, he took his rod and pushed it down to maybe get a little help from a push. The water was so deep that he ended up grabbing the rod by the tip while pushing it straight down and he never hit bottom. He never got on the rock and it almost killed him trying, thus the name "Tombstone Rock" came to be. To this day no one has ever gotten onto that rock as far as I know.

PHYSICAL CONDITIONING

When you make a commitment like going to an island to fish for a few days or a week or more, where you are delving into a good quality fishery like either one of these, make sure you are physically ready. In the month or two leading up to your trip it would behoove you to get in shape. Walking is a great way to condition, but also working on your upper body strength will aid you greatly. Push yourself and make it hurt, then when you get out to the island you can really enjoy the full experience with minimal fatigue. Fishing can be physically demanding, especially when the fishing is good. Make the most of your time!

RESPECT

One of the things I take very serious is respect for other people and for their property and their privacy. When walking late at night I have strict rules: no swinging lights or shining them on people's houses. Korker's or cleats on? Walk on the grass, not on the asphalt or sidewalks, because they crunch very loudly.

I strongly suggest minimal talking in the wee hours. On the islands most homes don't have air conditioning because they don't need it, so they sleep with their windows open and enjoy the cool night air. When you give respect you get respect, and that is a good way to go.

TICKS AND POISION IVY

As I preach to the point of annoyance, scouting is essential, it has to be done. When out walking the trails in your regular clothes you must pay attention for ticks. Ticks are a problem on both islands. The other thing you need to watch for and be mindful of is poison ivy. "Leaflet three, let it be." When you

Scouting is essential to good fishing. While out hunting for good water always keep watch for ticks and poison ivy, they both abound on both islands. Always carry bug spray and don't be afraid to use it!

are walking the trails with waders or wetsuit, you need not worry, but when walking the trails in shorts or sweatpants, pay attention, and take precautions. Use tick/mosquito repellant and check yourself thoroughly upon completion.

EQUIPMENT

When it comes to choosing equipment to fish the islands I would say if you are serious about the fishing and doing it the right way in search of a big bass, then you need to bring the big stuff. By that I mean a 10–11 foot rod, with a matching reel filled up with 30–40 pound test braid. On one cast you can get a 24-inch bass, three casts later it could be a 30-pound bass, you never know but you are out in the ocean where the big girls swim. If you want to go a little lighter I would say go with a 9-foot rod but one that has some backbone just in case you tie into a lulu.

Leader Material

For the large majority of my fishing I use 80-pound test monofilament leader material on either island. Why? Why not? Stripers are not leader shy in any way. The 80-pound test is tough, and forgiving on the rocky shoreline where you have fish that will run into the rocks as a means of escape. Mussel shells, lobster pots, barnacles, and other sharp object have no mercy on light line. The other reason I go heavy when wetsuiting is you are reeling your fish in to your feet and then you grab the leader to control the fish, and the 80-pound is a lot easier on your hands than 30-pound leader would be!

Lights

As a striped bass fisherman, the majority of your fishing is done in the dark, making lights very important for many reasons. Basically I carry two lights on my neck and at least one other in my plugbag. I personally prefer neck lights over head lamps. I have two different lights. One is a very powerful dive light—the one I use projects 220 lumens of light. This light will cut the night in half. I use it for finding rocks in the dark, checking my water for lobster pot ropes or buoys, or finding a hooked fish as it gets close. I call it this light the "doubt remover"—if you are not sure what's out there, you use it. The other light I wear is a very low-lumen light, perhaps around 10–15 lumens, and I Sharpie the lens green. This light is for lighting up anything from my plugbag to my feet and that is all it is good for. The green light helps protect my night vision. I attach my lights with surgical tubing and electrical tape. In my plugbag I carry a third light which works as a backup and it also becomes my "walking light." I use it when I need to light my path, as it saves the batteries of my good lights. Now I know I don't need to say this but I will—be sure you have fresh batteries in your lights, don't gamble in this category. Getting stuck with no light on these islands can be very unnerving, especially on a new moon! And remember, all lights have to be waterproof!

Waderbelt

You must always wear a waderbelt and pliers with a lanyard whenever and wherever you fish, always. If you don't wear a plugbag over your shoulder, you can then add pouches or plugbags to your belt as needed. I personally wear all my bags on my belt.

Knife

It is important for me to mention that for the surfcaster the need to carry a knife is important as you never know what lies beneath the surface, especially at night. Lobster pot lines can wreak havoc on you, and so can discarded braid left by an irresponsible fisherman. It is important to have a knife and to have the right knife—do not carry a fillet knife or a knife with any kind of a point. You want a stainless blunt-nose dive knife. Strap it on somewhere or carry it in your bag but have one ready and accessible at all times. You never know!

Having good quality equipment with you is essential when you are out fishing on these islands. Good lights, pliers, and cleated soles are extremely important. Notice the mung on the line and everywhere.

Footwear

When walking the rocks of the islands, protection and comfort are important as well as efficiency. A simple pair of wading boots without a clumsy cleated sandal attached is so comfortable to walk with. It's all I wear anymore. I wear wading boots with some sort of screws put in the soles to help me with traction on slippery rocks. The absolute best boot set-up will have felt soles and Grip Studs (available online). I prefer the #1500. A low profile exposure, with the tip protruding out less than an eighth of an inch works best. Do not use a long shaft screw as you run the risk of it going through the sole of your boot and that is torture when walking the rocks, trust me! A short, wide base is best. Also keep in mind that you want to look for a boot that has a thick sole on it, ¾ of an inch or more. The thick sole is good for two reasons, one is it works as a good base for the studs. Second, is it gives your foot added support as you walk on numerous uneven rocks that can really contort and mangle your feet.

Bug Spray

There is one small thing that will add an incredible amount of happiness and contentment to your time fishing on the islands—bug spray. Buy a lot and stow it with you. I buy the spray cans and I also grab Skin So Soft, or the equivalent (whatever is on sale) and as I am gearing up for the night, I slather the back of my neck, in my ears, and face and the back of my hands. Any exposed skin areas. I do several applications. Mosquitos drive me insane! I also carry a small travel-sized spray bottle of the liquid which I keep in my plugbag at all times.

LURES FOR THE ISLANDS

When I started fishing Cuttyhunk, Block, and other destinations where you are on the road and have little or no access to good tackle shops and such, I would over-pack and bring a ridiculous amount of plugs with me. I always feared that the one plug I left home would be the hot plug that I needed for the trip. Then you go on the trip and you use three lures the whole time while the other 300 sit rotting in the trays. I guess as time moves forward and you continue to learn, you simplify. I am a very strong believer that it is much more important to find fish where they are feeding, and then throwing any offering to them, as opposed to trying to rack my brain to make a choice on what lure to throw. Bass hunt in schools, where there is one fish there are ten or twenty fish, they are all hungry and they feed competitively, do you think that once feeding, they say to themselves, "ahhh I was looking for something a little bigger or smaller," or "I was looking for a darker shade of yellow tonight?" No, they hit anything that moves! If one fish doesn't eat it the one next to it certainly will. So you hunt and scout and scout and hunt for places where bass feed. Then lure choice gets easier. Once you find fish that are feeding it doesn't matter as much what you throw.

These are the lures that I would be sure to have with me when I go to either one of these islands.

- A loaded Red Fin.
- A Daiwa SP Minnow or equal.
- A 2-ounce pencil or Polaris popper.
- A 3-ounce pencil or Polaris popper.

- A 2-ounce wood needlefish.
- A 2⅜-ounce Super Strike needlefish.
- A 2⅜-ounce Super Strike darter.
- Bucktails: 1, 1½, 2 ounces.
- Otter Tails—long straight, cut to size.
- Rubber/leadhead combo: 1 and 1½ ounce heads.
- A 2–3 ounce tin.
- 5-inch Yo-Zuri Mag-Darter.

Island Line Up Part One. From top to bottom: The 3-ounce Super Strike Little Neck Popper, can also be a Gibbs 3½-ounce Polaris popper. The 2½-ounce Striper Maine-iac Pencil, the 3 ounce Goo-Goo Man Pencil, Goo-Goo Man 2¾-ounce metal lip swimmer, Striper Maine-iac's 2¾-ounce Atom A-40, and Afterhours 2¾-ounce Danny.

My starting lineup for the islands would look something like this. The loaded Red Fin, loaded (weighted) Super Strike needle, 2 ounce wood needle, 2–3 ounce pencil poppers, bucktails with Otter Tails, leadheads with rubber. Everything after this becomes second or third option or experimental.

The loaded Red Fin could be switched out for a Daiwa SP Minnow if you change all the hardware on it. The Daiwa SP Minnow out of the package does not have hooks or split rings strong enough to hold big bass. The splits and hooks have to be upsized either way. This lure covers your upper column with a decent-sized offering. It has been very good to me in terms of catching fish. The weighted Super Strike needle, a great lure for extending your range while getting good penetration at the same time, makes an invaluable weapon to tote! The 2-ounce wood needle, good casting, always on or near the surface with the long and skinny profile. The pencil popper, another great casting, distance lure that wakes the dead and draws curious, distant bass to within range. The pencil has accounted for many nice bass for me on both islands. It is one of my go-to lures for sure. The bucktail with an Otter Tail trailer, or the leadhead with a rubber, is probably my top catcher. This covers the bottom half of my water column where most of the big bass hang out as they hunt the shallows for crabs and lobsters and a feed on the plethora of bait fish that are moving through.

What you throw after that becomes more specific based on certain conditions or certain baits that may present themselves to you. One of my favorites from the next level down are big Danny's or A-40's, especially in the boulderfields. There is nothing better than watching your swimmer come kicking around a boulder only to see a nice bass come up under it and blowing it out of the water before devouring it!

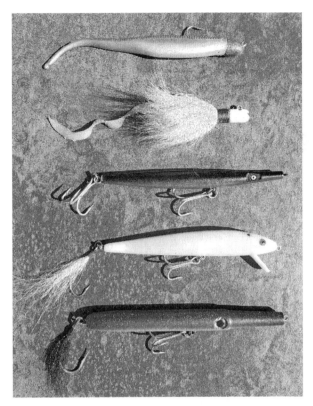

Island Line Up Part Two. Top to bottom. My all-time favorite big bass lure, the 9" Mega-Shad with a 1 or 1½-ounce leadhead. The timeless bucktail, again 1 to 1½ ounce in most normal situations, the weighted Super Strike N-Fish (needle), a Cotton Cordell loaded Red Fin (loaded with bird shot), and one of my favorite needles, the 2-ounce Hab's—blurple has been good to me through the years.

CHAPTER TWO

Block Island:
Introduction and Overview

Block Island is located off the coast of Rhode Island, and was named after Dutch explorer Adriaen Block. It is located in the Atlantic Ocean about 14 miles east of Montauk Point, New York, and 13 miles south of mainland Rhode Island. Martha's Vineyard and Cuttyhunk Island are approximately 35 miles north and east of Block Island, as the crow flies (or in this case the sea gull). You can get to Block Island using the Steamship Authority ferry from Point Judith, Rhode Island. (This is the main ferry to Block Island. There are a couple of other, smaller operations that only carry passengers.) The ferry takes vehicles and passengers and the ride takes about an hour. I would strongly suggest that if a summer fishing trip to Block is in the stars, you make your vehicle reservations in March or early April. It also has a very nice airport (a great place for breakfast) with flights coming and going all the time. Block Island makes up the town of New Shoreham, the smallest town in the smallest state.

Block Island is almost six miles long, top to bottom, and about three and a half miles wide at its widest point. The island offers rolling hills and large wooded areas interspersed

Block Island's beautiful Southeast Light was built in 1873. It was moved back from the edge of the eroding bluff in 1993 to where it sits today.

with farms that have been cleared through the years. Many stone walls add to the island's beauty. Only the main roads are paved and the rest of the roads are dirt. To fish Block correctly you will spend a lot of time on the dirt roads. Besides the fishing there is plenty for people to do with biking, hiking trails, beaches, clamming, relaxing, and enjoying the beach environment. In the summer the place is mobbed with tourists, sailing people, and people looking to have drinks, listen to music, and go to the beach. When it isn't summer the place is calm, quiet and a beautiful place to be. The striped bass just adds to its magic.

As a fisherman on Block I would strongly suggest that you go to The Star Department Store, directly across from the ferry, and buy one of their excellent maps of the island. This map is very comprehensive and detailed. You can also go to

Twin Maples apartments and tackle shop on Beach Road, say hello and ask them for one of their maps of the island and see if you can get any recent fishing reports. For the sake of being thorough, I would get one from both places. Twin Maples is one of the two tackle shops on Block, and it has a limited amount of resources, but certainly enough to supply your needs. The other shop is Fishworks, located on Ocean Avenue near New Harbor. It is not a big shop, but boy is it well stocked and the guys are always very helpful. Most important, both places have eels! Block Island is to me what a playground is to a five-year-old. It offers plenty of fish, and many different terrains that give you plenty of options on where to fish. This variety also allows you to use many different techniques. It has the awesome boulderfields to the east and south, and has the sand beaches on the west side. It offers one of the great rips at Sandy Point, and it has two inlets, both man-made, Old Harbor on the east side and the Coast Guard Channel (New Harbor) on the west side.

Block has something to offer everyone. For the angler who wants to go for a week, have some fun, put on the waders and get lost in a hunt for schoolies around the island, it is there for him. Even the most marginal bass hunter can be satisfied on Block. The island also offers great porgy and fluke fishing from shore. For someone looking for some relaxing daytime fishing, hit the Coast Guard Channel with some squid or Gulp baits. For the cow hunter, who is seldom seen in the daylight hours and dons the wetsuit, Block can also be a place of great solace and challenge. It will give up some monster fish for those that go deep, think things through carefully, and work the night tides hard.

One of the fun parts of wetsuiting is getting on your rock, but if you aren't quick enough this is what happens. It looks much worse than it is.

One of the beautiful things about fishing Block Island is the relatively easy access to countless fishing spots. You can really be mobile on the "pork chop" (as the island is called, owing to its shape), hitting many different spots in a night. It is a lot of driving and plenty of dusty roads, but they all add to good fishing opportunities. It may take you a little time to figure out how to get everywhere, especially if you are new to the island, but once you do you can get lost in the fishing. On Block you can easily fish several spots a night for a week straight and never fish the same spot twice—it is loaded with great spots. I would suggest that you first spend a lot of time looking for good water or scouting for irresistible spots, some of which we'll be talking about shortly. Find areas that look good and that give you confidence! Fish those areas hard.

Don't get lulled into the trap of fishing where people who fished the island long ago want you to—scout out good water for yourself. Remember too that you need to hunt for bodies of fish along with good water. The fish move around the island and hold in certain areas for periods of time before they move on. Again, we'll be discussing this phenomenon in more detail a bit later in this book.

WIND AND TIDE

You need to learn about tides and their effect on current direction wherever you are fishing on the island, especially in conjunction with the factor of wind direction. Generally on Block Island, the incoming tide moves north to south down the sides of the island. You always want to fish wind with tide, never wind against tide. If you cast a lure out (I usually use a Red Fin) and reel it back in, if it comes straight in and there is no sweep caused by current, there is no use fishing that spot—there is not enough water movement to get bait and bass active. If you have a hard north wind and you are fishing the incoming tide, you are going to have good water movement until the tide turns. On a south wind you would have problems on the incoming tide because you would have wind against tide. Much also depends on how hard the wind is blowing, so it can get a little complicated. That is why it's important to pay attention and keep a journal that tells you the tide or stage of the tide you fished, wind direction and speed. The tides can be unpredictable on Block—in fact there are a couple of spots where the tide seems to pull in one direction all the time.

You have to remember that Block is out there in the Atlantic and it is always getting hit with big ocean currents, and those currents can drive you crazy when you are trying to figure out a particular direction in a specific spot on a certain tide.

MY FISHING ON BLOCK

I have fished Block Island extensively and it has given me everything that I could have asked for! I love the challenges that it offers.

I had the good fortune of fishing Block for two weeks straight a few years back and I was able to track bodies of bass to learn how they moved around. Upon arrival and as always in a new location, I first scouted the entire area, or island in this case. Then I began fishing by visiting a couple of reliable spots to get a feel for what was going on. It usually doesn't take long to figure out what is happening. The first considerable body of fish I found was at Sandy Point (see map on page 64). I had the wind and tide moving in the same direction and my small group had a solid hit of fish for two nights, most fish ranging from 30 inches up to about 18 pounds, and then the hit petered out. It was time to see which way the bass had gone—did they head down the west side of the island along the sand beaches towards the Coast Guard Channel, a never-ending bait supply, or did they go down the rocky east side into big bass territory? Notice that just because I had two fabulous nights at Sandy Point to start, I did not stay there the entire time. As good as it was, the fish had moved on so it was time for me to move on as well. Up-sizing was definitely on my mind too. When fishing rips like Sandy Point and you are into a solid hit of fish, and let's say the fish are smaller, under 20 pounds, that does not necessarily mean that the bigger bass are not there, but that they may be just slightly further out in deeper or more turbid water. I wanted to ascertain which way this body of fish went, did they head down the west and south or did they go east, or did they split completely? I love rocky boulderfields, no matter where they are, and I gravitate to them, so naturally my instinct pushed me east to find these fish. My crew and I hit several spots on the east side over about a five-mile stretch, from Grove Point, along Isaiah's Notch clear down to The Poop Chute (locals give it a more explicit name), and my guess was apparently wrong as we settled for a less-than-desirable effort for the night. My wrong guess was exacerbated when I ran into some of my fly-fishing buddies who proceeded to tell me that they had a great night at Charleston Beach (just outside and south of the Coast Guard Channel) with fish up to and over 25 pounds consistently. Naturally the next night we worked the west side. Not Charleston of course, because I was sure the fly guys would be looking for an encore and I wouldn't want to step on them by showing up there with three or four other fishermen. So we hit Grace's Cove first, just south of Charleston, where we were rewarded again with some good fishing. We worked our way down into Dories, having fish wherever we stopped, and I knew this was the body of fish we had at Sandy Point. This hit continued for another night before slowing. My next guess was that these fish would move further south towards Southwest Point, maybe Schooner Point or around to Black Rock Point. I licked my chops as now the fish were moving into my wheelhouse, the area of

Black Rock, Barlow's, Great Point and Snake Hole, where I knew we also had the chance of running into some of the bigger mommies. Throw into the mix that I got a solid tip from a boat guy who said they caught some 50-pound-class fish tight to the beach at Southwest, and my next move was an easy decision. I felt really confident with the plan, and felt pretty good thinking that one of us had a good shot at one of the Block Island giants. I had the "body" locked down . . . or so I thought. I and three other guys spread out over about a mile and a half of boulders at dusk and fished long into the night. The result was a rare happening, especially on Block, but the night produced four goose eggs. How do you like that? As soon as you think you've got it all figured out. . . . I usually try to keep my expectations in check, never too low or too high. This time I had them high and the letdown hurt, leaving me scratching my head about this amazing fish. Out-maneuvered again!

So it was back to the drawing board. I checked in with the fly guys again and they again had a good shot the previous night, followed by a big slowdown, so my next logical move was back north to Sandy Point. Boo-yah! We had good fishing once again, confirming that the night previous was the wrong move as the fish moved back north, as opposed to the south side of the island. I wouldn't have guessed that in a hundred guesses. We had two very good nights, then another slow-down which I would label it as a slow pick and another move was in order. But which way this time?

I was now into week number two and I had watched these fish move from north to west, towards south, turn around

Many nights we fed them a steady diet of loaded Red Fins and loaded Super Strike needles. Those are two of my Block Island heavy hitters.

to the west and then finally back to the north tip yet again. The fish were familiar and it was the same body of fish that I had picked up on day one, the only thing that was missing was the big ones and that was about to change. My next guess was again to the boulders (see? I'm a sucker for the boulders). This time there were six of us, which allowed me to range a lot further than I normally would. We spread out over a two-mile stretch from Pots and Kettles down to Old Harbor on the east side and it was game on! For the next two nights we had our same body of hungry fish but this time they were joined by some bigger fish, along with good numbers on mid-teen to mid-20 pound class fish. We took some 30- and 40-pound class bass and it felt really good. We had the big fish showing and joining our other body, it had to happen based on the fact that the migration was still under way and fish were moving, the travelers were still showing up or passing through, and in this case the new arrivals were hogs.

I finished the trip with solid fishing, making it a complete success. The spring calendar was moving into summer, with more migrating fish continuing to show up, allowing for some serious Block Island fishing. I finished the trip catching fish almost at will and wherever we set up. We were fishing until we were exhausted and waking up late and looking for something quick, hot, and delicious, refocusing on what a new plan and a new night would bring us. Good times for sure!

One of the things that allowed us to move and set up in so many different spots was because we knew those spots. That is why I want to emphasize to you to learn your access points early on and learn how to fish each spot. Different spots fish differently—coves fish different from points and inlets fish different from the boulderfields. Throw in variations of tides and wind and the need to prepare and plan in advance is obvious.

Big bass are landed on Block Island each year, making it a place of legend. Putting in long hours in the dark produces great fish that are immediately released after a couple of quick photos and a weigh session.

Eight Straight

At another time I was fishing Block hard and I was on the backend of eight consecutive all-nighters. I was having a hard time getting accommodations on the island—$250 bucks a night simply wasn't an option. So some buddies and I got a room at the Lighthouse Inn over on the mainland, across the street from the Block Island Ferry. I took my truck over to the island and left it there. We would take the ferry over around five in the afternoon and then I would go get my Xterra and we would head off to the happy hunting grounds. Normally when I fish, I like to start at dusk, like 7 p.m., and fish until the tide craps out, and then head in or maybe move to a different spot. By 2 or 3 a.m. you are good, you have a couple of beers and you are ready for the rack! Well when you have no rack, you just keep fishing, what else are you going to do? The first ferry off the island is at 8 a.m., so we were fishing 10–12 hours a night! I would pray for sunrise. Sunrise meant the flood of light, which meant the end of fishing as the fish move offshore when the sun comes up. As soon as the fireball popped up, I would look for the softest pile of rocks I could find and try to rest until it was time to get to the ferry. Now in a hotel room with three or four guys and a couple of air mattresses there is no such thing as good sleep. Try doing that three or four nights in a row. . . . OK now make that eight. Not terribly smart.

It was night Number Eight and I was completely shot out. There were two things that I distinctly remember about that night. One was how tired I was, the fatigue hanging on me like a huge wet sleeping bag. Concentration level: extremely low. I was dozing off in mid-retrieve, fighting hard just to stay awake! It was one of the few times that I actually fell asleep standing up. The problem is that when you fall asleep standing up, you fall down. I woke up when I hit the rock and water and bubbleweed. I landed on my rod and ground it against the boulder—thank goodness I didn't land on my reel! My rod was all scratched up and the back of my hand was bleeding a little. I got back up on my rock. I looked over to check on my two buddies and I saw their two silhouettes in the darkness, then went back to casting. I was so tired! It was shortly thereafter that the second thing that I distinctly remember about that night took place.

I was fishing one of my trusty loaded Red Fins, of course it was painted green, after all it was Block! (For some unknown reason the color Block Island green, which is an almost fluorescent green, is a very popular color on Block Island and has been since the 80s. I'm not sure if it is just a trendy pick that has become "the" color or if it really is a color that bass prefer or see better while around Block Island.) Anyway my Fin was halfway in and I was fighting hard to stay awake and not nod off. Then she came calling—a sudden sharp strike, I instinctively came back hard and suddenly the drag screamed. "Oh boy," I thought, "This is a good fish!"

Now when you get tight to a good fish, everything in your body goes full bore, your blood is flowing, your heart is pumping, the adrenaline has you jacked up. Well Mr. Numbnut here just wanted it to be over, I was so tired. It was a good fish and I fought it for more than five minutes. During my battle I decided that since I was so pooped I didn't care if I landed it or not, I just wanted to see its size. I worked the fish and as it got close I grabbed my necklight, hit the button on the light, and BOOM the fish was gone. Where I should have been angry or dejected I was actually happy. I was so tired I didn't care. I went back in to shore, back to my truck where I sat down and dozed off to another place. When I got home from Block I was checking some reports when I got wind of a fifty taken on Block a few nights prior. What?! I was just there! How could this be? Twin Maples had given the report and I knew John fairly well so I called him to check on it. To make a long story short, I found out that there was a big fish caught that night and it was over 50 pounds. I started to run the scenario of what happened that night in my mind. Big bass on the beach doesn't happen all the time but that night they were obviously there. I had one on and passed on it because I was pooped. Needless to say that once I got some legitimate rest and did some reflection, my emotions fell more on where they should have been, angry with myself and frustrated at my error of pushing myself to the point of apathy. I learned a very valuable lesson and I paid a high price for it.

CHAPTER THREE

Fishing Block Island

Now I will take you clockwise around the island. I will describe each locale and comment on it. Please remember that these structures or locations can change from year to year, storm to storm. What you have one year you may not have again the next year. Remember to scout as much as you can.

SANDY POINT

Sandy Point is the north tip of the pork chop and it is where the waters of Block Island Sound and the Atlantic Ocean collide after being swept around the island. When the tide is pulling, the rip continues out for as far as the eye can see. (A rip is a long seam where currents collide, making for great fishing as baitfish lose control in the violent water.) I consider it one of the best rips on the East Coast and it is one of the places that I really look forward to when fishing the Block. When the tide is really pulling you cast out to the left at nine o'clock and you reel it in at three. Now that's a rip! As you cast out and let your lure sink you will feel the rocks below. Ba ba-ba ba-ba . . . THUD! The strikes are hard and unmistakable! One of my

BLOCK ISLAND

1. SANDY POINT
2. COW COVE
3. GROVE POINT
4. BALL'S NORTH POINT
5. POTS AND KETTLES
6. MANSION BEACH
7. CRESCENT BEACH
8. OLD HARBOR
9. BALLARD'S BEACH
10. OLD HARBOR POINT
11. SOUTHEAST LIGHT
12. THE STEPS
13. MOHEGAN BLUFFS
14. PAINTED ROCK/SNAKE HOLE
15. BLACK ROCK POINT
16. SCHOONER POINT
17. SOUTHWEST POINT
18. DORIE'S COVE
19. GRACE'S POINT
20. CHARLESTON BEACH
21. COAST GUARD CHANNEL
22. THE DUMP
23. CORN NECK ROAD
24. NEW HARBOR
25. CLAYHEAD TRAIL

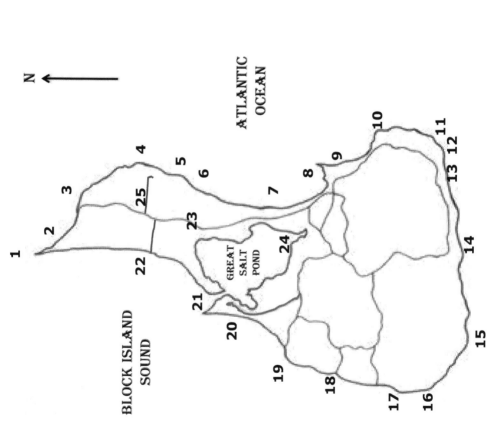

N

ATLANTIC OCEAN

BLOCK ISLAND SOUND

GREAT SALT POND

favorite times to fish here, besides any time, is in the fall when the winds are howling out of the northwest, the harder the better, the place lights up real nice! In the fall the place can be hot day or night, definitely worth the 15–20 minute walk from the parking lot. Don't be surprised when you pull a big ugly yellow-eye out of here either. Bluefish like it here and they are a great fight in the rip!

When it comes to choosing what tide to fish here, I have always fished the point on the outgoing tide. You must remember that the tide here is different from what the tide chart says. I give it an extra two or two and a half hours before heading out. So if slack tide is at 12, I won't go out until 2–2:30.

At Sandy Point I like to cast heavy offerings. One reason is the added distance a heavier lure will get you, which is

Sandy Point offers one of the best rips on the East coast, especially in the fall when the wind howls out of the northwest on the outgoing tide.

sometimes essential to reaching fish. Another reason is penetration through the water column—you need to feel the lure bouncing off the rocky bottom. I usually lean upon my bucktails and a trailer/strip like an Otter Tail, which is my go-to trailer. As for lure weight, it will depend on how hard the current is moving, but I start at 1½ ounces and then move up as necessary. I like the bucktails too if bluefish are present, as I would rather they mess with a bucktail rather than biting the tail off one of my good soft baits! Another favorite option of mine here is throwing either one of my custom-loaded Super Strike needles (the heavier the better) or one of my custom-loaded Cotton Cordell pencil poppers, loaded up to 3-plus ounces, which I originally loaded for fishing the Cape Cod Canal. (I often load lures with bird shot to give them extra weight.) The loaded pencil is to be fished deep, along the bottom, not in the traditional manner. The weight gives me adequate distance and much needed penetration.

One autumn afternoon the rip was white and wild and at about 70 yards there was a dark green strip cutting through the whitewater. Every time I hit that trough, I had a nice bass or big ugly blue. The Super Strike needles I like to load up to around 2.7–3 ounces, and I like these very much when I am fighting hard cross winds as they get out and then down quickly. The Super Strike Bullet, loaded up, also shines here. I can do whatever I want to with that lure! As usual I am fishing these with a single tail hook and a 3/0 4X treble on the belly attached by a 5.5H split ring.

There will be times when you have to change your casting angles to try to find where the fish are holding. Sometimes they are more out towards the left at 10 or 11 o'clock while at other times you may need to cast out more to the right, 12 or one o'clock and then let it sweep.

Sandy Point Safety

You must be very, very careful when wading out onto the sand bar! Fishermen have drowned at Sandy Point. As you will see when you get there, you will have water hitting you from two directions and sometimes from behind. *Go only out to mid-shin depth!* When out there with good moving water or a moon tide, always throw an occasional glance behind you as floating trees and logs will often get swept over that bar, so be aware. If you are shin deep it shouldn't be a problem. This is a lot more common on big (high) moon tides.

COW COVE

Moving clock-wise around the island we first come to Cow Cove. Cow Cove is the long cove you see when looking left from the parking lot at Settlers Rock up past North Light. Cow Cove leads right to Sandy Point. If you scouted it you

The view from Grove Point looking west along Cow Cove as it swings past North Light towards Sandy Point.

would find nothing of interest, but don't be fooled by the tranquil, structure-less appearance and don't walk by it without at least making a couple of casts to keep it honest. I know that some very big stripers have come out of this area, including one bass over 50 pounds caught on a live eel along this stretch and several other nice fish caught that same night. I began to fish it with a little more intent after that news and did surprisingly well despite nothing notable there to hold fish. I think that possibly the fish that work the rip at Sandy Point may come down into Cow Cove to rest in calmer water for a spell, making it a spot worth hitting. It can be very productive around high water.

GROVE POINT

This place I call the "Northeast Corner," basically because it is the northeast corner. You park at the top of Corn Neck Road at Settler's Rock and walk east or to the right. As you walk you will see Grove Point Rock sitting out off the beach a couple of hundred yards. Keep walking and soon the bluff will rise on your right and you are getting into some good striper terrain. I have caught some beautiful fish here on my favorite, leadhead-rubbers. The water pulls nicely around this corner, left to right on the incoming tide. I prefer wetsuiting this spot by getting out and finding one of the "pedestal" rocks as I call them, since this spot has two or three tall, skinny rocks that look like pedestals While pushing out a bit can put you into some heavyweight fish, one night I happened across a couple of 30-pounders while standing on the cobbles. I was walking back from points further south and casting as I went. Well sure enough I hit a couple of mid- to upper 30-pound fish. I marked the spot because in the dark you lose some concept of where you are. The next morning I went back and found my mark and saw that I had caught the fish between the pedestals and the beach, which surprised me because I was unknowingly casting to the area behind the Pedestals. It goes to show that these fish are not afraid of shallow water at night.

This area is a good darter area, a good eel area, or a good leadhead/rubber spot. It offers some very good current sweep.

BALL'S POINT

Now from the "Northeast Corner" south is a very long cove which is named Isaiah's Gully. At the end you find Ball's North, Ball's, and Pots and Kettles, an area known as Clay Head. Clay Head because if you look up at the bluffs you can see a lot of layers of clay in the numerous layers of geological swaths. When heavy rains assault the island, it washes a lot of clay into the water, dirtying up the shallows and making them unfishable. This happens a lot around the island in bad weather.

When fishing these great points I like to push out onto the points and find a good, big, flat rock that gives me access to deep water, then I do my thing. Usually the same recipe, pencils at dusk and dawn and rubber and bucktails in the dark. If you find a spot with deep water in front of you, eels should be considered as big fish often pay visits to these spots.

POTS AND KETTLES/ MANSION BEACH

This stretch of beach here, also known as a part of Clay Head, offers some great-looking structure, sand and boulders. You can get to this point by parking in the Clay Head Nature Trail lot and taking a walk through the woods until you get to the ocean. The majority of this terrain is sandy beaches strewn with boulders—the points especially are boulder-strewn and gorgeous. Most of the good structure is to the left or north. The wetsuit guys will want to get out and fish some of those points, while the wader-wearer can work this stretch by walking the sandy coves, in either direction, especially after dark, and casting to the edges of the points. The water here is usually flat and calm as the prevailing wind on Block is southwest and the wind will be over the shoulder. Poppers are effective anytime. This is a place where I would throw needles and sandeel and spearing imitations, such as the Diawa SP Minnows and similar baits. Don't rule out teasers either.

Clay Head Trail leads to Pots and Kettles, pictured here. Sandy beaches with boulders scattered everywhere—super structure. This is looking south towards Old Harbor.

CRESCENT BEACH/BALLARD'S/THE CHUTE

There are a couple of places on Block that I don't commit a lot of time to, one of those is the stretch from Mansion Beach down along Crescent Beach to the harbor. Crescent Beach seems fairly uninteresting to me from a surfcasting perspective. It offers a lot of sand and a gradual, sloping beach. When I am on Block I am forever called to the beautiful boulderfields and to the structure, the vibrant ecosystems, and to the deep water access that the boulderfields offer. So does this stretch produce? Everything produces at times, but the best of this stretch is hands down Ballard's down to the Chute. A simple look at the beach at Ballard's and you will see the structure, large boulders strewn about a sandy bottom. The problem is that at night in the warm months the parties at Ballard's get very loud with music and drunken people! At other times it may be worth a shot. The Chute, at one time the sewer outflow for Block, holds tons of bait and tons of life, definitely worth a few casts as long as you have cleats fast to the soles of your boots.

OLD HARBOR POINT

Now we are moving into some serious striper terrain. From Old Harbor Point to Black Rock Point is quite possibly the best striper terrain in the world. I would like to hear arguments to the contrary. Old Harbor Point and it's adjacent structure offers good water movement and good water depth. Big bass can move in close here.

To get to this area you park on Spring Street near the Chute overlooking the cove beside the point. Hop over the guardrail,

Old Harbor Point (far point) offers great bass fishing, and the waters leading out aren't so bad either.

down the rip-rap to the beach. You can fish this entire area and do well just about any time, although of course the large majority of the fishing should be done at night.

At Old Harbor I like to throw the standards, pencil poppers anytime, and then darters, needles, rubber/leadheads and loaded Red Fins. This is also a great eeling spot.

SOUTHEAST LIGHT

The rocky shoreline beneath Southeast Light running back north towards Old Harbor Point offers world-class structure and seemingly endless bouldery points. Any of the areas under the light are, in my humble estimation, as good as it gets.

Getting to this area will take a bit of an effort. To access it you will need to hit "The Steps." The Steps are dreaded, not so much for the walk down as for the walk up! At some point along the line some physical fitness conditioning would be helpful before you get to Block and this is one of the reasons why! I think the last time I counted there were 131 steps but I think that changes year to year or even storm to storm.

Once at the bottom of the stairs, most go left. From this point you have access to great striped bass opportunities. I have caught good bass all over this stretch. My suggestion is to scout, scout, scout for good water. The terrain can change quite a bit over the winter due to colossal winter storms and pounding Atlantic surf. A rock that you had last year may be long gone when you return the next year. Now by good water I mean find good rocks to access out on the end of the points, you want to find good pulling, deep water within casting distance. You will recognize great water by simply looking for

The rocky shoreline that sits beneath Southeast Light offers some of the best striper fishing on the planet. Bouldery points accompanied by deep coves help draw big fish that hunt in the rocks.

water that you see physically moving left to right or right to left in front of you. Look for seams or creases, which make it even more appealing because that is where you have water currents colliding. The bigger the seam or the faster the water, the better! The other thing you want to find is deep water, the deeper water will draw your big fish in tight. Deep water can be recognized simply as dark water when looking from above or from afar.

As you continue to walk the coves and points you will just keep refreshing yourself with great looking water and endless striper opportunities.

At the bottom of the stairs and to the right, there are a couple of massive boulders surrounded by smaller boulders on a point. This area also offers some very deep water in front of it. Looking at it you will see great bass terrain, and it would

Stairway to Heaven? Quite possibly! If you walk down the stairs and fish to the left you will be in some seriously good bass water. The terrain is rocks and boulders and there will be plenty of points and coves to keep you happy.

behoove you to fish it, but beware of bluefish as they like this spot for some reason too. Moving further right you have a long sandy stretch that will get you to Great Point, a good walk-and-cast area in low light conditions.

SNAKE HOLE

The next easy access point is Snake Hole Road. The famous Block Island landmark, the Painted Rock, will let you know that you have arrived at your turn. This rock has been painted thousands of times, often numerous times a day in the summer months. I often joke that is started out as a pebble that was one inch long.

You drive down to the end of Snake Hole Road and park on the left somewhere. Walk down a culvert through the

The famous Painted Rock. When I began fishing Block, this rock was the size of a milk crate. In the summer it often gets painted three to four times a day.

woods to the water and you will come out at Snake Hole, a deep-water cove. To your right you will see a big point called Barlow's Point and to your left you will see Vail Beach. Again a lot of very good striper terrain. Snake Hole is deep and needs to be probed as it draws and holds some very big bass. Rubber/leadheads, bucktails, swimmers and loaded needles do well here.

BLACK ROCK POINT

Black Rock Point has always been one of my favorite points for catching stripers. It is again a place that if you made up some structure in your mind, building it perfectly, this point is what you would come up with. It also has a small point to its left where I have done well, called Tom's Point. If you walk past Black Rock Point and keep walking to the next point you will hit a point that I have never seen anyone else fish, called Lewis Point. I have done well there and since it is a place that receives very little pressure you may get a slight edge on unsuspecting bass.

Big bass can be found all around Block Island, but if you fish the waters of the southeast side you should be prepared for some real heavyweights.

SOUTHWEST POINT

The first time I saw Southwest Point I was surprised by its lack of structure. After all the hype and folklore I had heard about it, I was expecting something quite different. It's really just a gravel bar, a low-profile pile of small rocks, and very difficult to stand on. You want to fish it on the outgoing tide, where the water moves left to right over top the bar and then dumps into a big cove to the right. As the tide moves it creates some wave action that rolls up on the point, enough to attract some fish. It fishes in an uncommon manner as I recall numerous nights where we definitely fished it on the outgoing and it was pulling left to right, yet when I spoke with Dennis Zambrotta he recalled the opposite on the outgoing, he would hook big fish in the cove to the right and fight it to the left with the tide. Strange! So I dug a little deeper and found out that it pulls right to left on the first part of the outgoing, and then left to right on the second half of the outgoing. As I have stated, these island tides can be befuddling! And it makes sense as historically I never fish Southwest Point until two hours into the outgoing. As with everything, a wind in the direction of your tide will only help you.

Once a place of great legend, Southwest Point is now just a shell of the great fishing it once delivered. While I have fished it extensively for years it has never given up any big fish to me. I have had nights with great numbers here, but never great size. That said, I hear repeatedly that the section of the island between Black Rock and Southwest gives up the biggest bass to the boat fishermen. But it has never translated into big fish for yours truly. One afternoon I heard from John at Twin Maples that several big bass, fifty-pound plus, were taken just off the beach there by boat guys so I pursued the tip that night and came up with a goose egg. What happens off the beach at Block usually stays off the beach at Block.

It was also at this spot where I had one of the strangest nights with my good friend and expert surfcaster Mark Jolliffe. We were out on the gravel bar, casting away, and I had the pattern figured out and was in a groove. Cast out behind the waves with a loaded Super Strike needle, let it sink for a few moments then catch up and start reeling very slow and BAM! Fish on! I was on the right side of the bar and Mark was on my left. I kept catching while Mark didn't. So after I have about 12 bass to his zero, I was getting concerned because he always adapts well. So I went over to check things out. He was throwing the same needle as me. I told him what I was doing in detail. I went back to casting. We are fishing away and now it was 15-0 and I can sense that he's getting a little frustrated, believe me I was too! So to be friendly, I go over, take his spot, take his lure and give him both my lure and my spot. My first cast with his lure in his spot BAM! I'm on again. I did it a few more times then I look over and no Mark. I look around in the dark and I call out to him—nothing. Weird! I walk in and see one of the other guys sitting there on a log and I ask him where Mark went. He said he came out ten minutes ago and went up to the truck. I felt terrible but there is nothing you can do about it. He was angry and frustrated to say the least. It is stuff like that, that makes me really scratch my head sometimes in this sport.

The easiest way to get to Southwest Point to go down all the way to the end of Cooneymus Road, park, walk onto the beach and go left for a few minutes out to the point that you see. (I am not going to lie, there is another way there but I know it only by sight and I have no idea the names of the dirt roads I drive on. It's a little complicated, so stick with the Cooneymus Road parking area and walk. It is not a long walk.)

Now if you keep walking past Southwest Point you come to a nice stretch of boulderfield where the water drops off pretty quick. I have had some good fishing in this area, better than at the Point. Keep walking some more and you come to Schooner Point, another well preserved hideaway seldom visited by surfcasters. Walk some more and you would end up at Dickens and then Lewis Point. This entire area is good fishing as long as the onshore wind doesn't dirty the water up too much.

DORRY'S COVE

Dorry's Cove is a good place to fish. Drive down to the end of Dorry's Cove Road and park, then walk onto the beach at the middle of the cove. It is quite different from the big, boulder-strewn ocean beaches to the east—much calmer. The cove itself is mostly sand and gravel. As you get out to either point it converts back more to rocks. You can go either right or left for a good time. If you walk to the left and get up to one of my favorite spots, Martin's Point, there are a couple of nice boulders right on the corner and this is a good spot to cast. The water usually moves nicely left to right on the outgoing, sweeping into the cove. The bass usually cooperate. I like penetration throughout the water column here, throwing bucktails, leadhead-rubbers, if they are not producing then maybe SP Minnows or loaded Red Fins high in the column. Really anything will work as long as the water is moving. Do yourself a favor here in the dark, take your powerful light and do a sweep of the water before you cast. See if you spot any lobster pot buoys, which usually have reflective tape on them. Several times I didn't check and lost good lures to the pots. (Why they drop them so damn close, I'll never know!) If you continue further to the left you will hit a big boulder-field. There have been times where the area produced nicely. By wading out as far as you could go and finding a rock you had a chance at some bigger fish, some years are good, some years nothing. It is why you have to actually get out and fish different areas all the time to find good bodies of fish. If you keep walking left you will end up at Southwest Point. (Don't do that, I am just telling you for reference.)

Now if you walk into the cove and go right to the point you will see a massive boulder. I call it the "Grand Stage" because it is like a big stage, and if you get on it you can perform some magic! This rock is not an easy rock to get on. You have to get around in front of it and crawl up onto it. The problem is that the water in front is very deep so you have to swim it. (As mentioned earlier, *do not try swimming onto a rock if you have not done it many times before and NEVER alone!*) Once you get on it you have a great perch for the night and you should have no problems pulling double digits. If you don't want to sweat the Grand Stage keep going a little further along the beach and you will find a promontory that juts out just a bit and you can find a nice rock to stand on. This entire area will produce all night long as the fish just keep cycling through, hunting for food in the shallows. If you keep walking this long stretch of boulders and sand, look for boulders out in waist-to neck-deep water, get on one and let the fun begin! For the most part this is not really deep water so you will do very well with your hard plastic swimmers, or rubber with lighter heads. Paddletail shads will also be effective.

Keep walking and soon you will hit Grace's Point.

GRACE'S POINT

If you drive down to the end of Grace's Cove Road and park you will walk out into Grace's Cove. Walk to the left and you will arrive at Grace's Point. The area you walk past on your way out will produce fish for you. If you can push out at all and even get onto a small rock, one that may only be big enough for your feet, you can do some damage. I lost a real nice fish here late one night that straightened my hooks. Once you get to the point proper, at lower levels of the tide there is a huge tabletop rock that will easily and comfortably hold two guys, at low tide you can wade to it, at high tide it is probably two to

The west side of the island is much calmer and has a lot more sand. Dorry's Cove and Grace's Point offer good fishing! This stretch usually gives up fairly good numbers and always a chance at an occasional big girl.

three feet underwater. If you can get to it you will have some great fishing, provided the fish are willing to entertain you for the night. Keep walking left some more and you will have to look for some boulders to go out and get on. It is a pretty straight run all the way down to Dorry's. This stretch is also a great wader-fishing area.

Many times I like to fish this backside area, Dorry's and Grace's, in the wee hours after spending the early evening fishing out front in the big water. I call it a "fallback" spot. It's a spot that you fall back to when you want to relax a bit but not stop fishing, when you still have some gas in the tank. These aren't big-fish spots, but you will occasionally hook a heavyweight female. Don't get lazy or you may get your heart broken.

If you walk to the right at Grace's, good luck. I have seldom fished this spot simply because it has never spoken to me, it just hasn't had the appeal that I am looking for when fishing Block Island. It seems to me to be shallow and shoaled out.

CHARLESTON BEACH

Just outside the Coast Guard Channel and running to the south is Charleston Beach, and just south of that is a long cove called Dead Man's Cove. This stretch is all sandy beach with very few if any rocks at all. While this beach looks uninspiring and wouldn't normally grab my attention, I know better. The only reason I know better is because when I used to stay at the Twin Maples in June each year, the fly guys from New Jersey would also be staying there and they would tell me of how good they were doing fishing Charleston. Catching bass up into the mid-20s was not uncommon for the fly boys. I never bothered to fish there while they were there but it was nice to know what was going on. If you look at this stretch on the map, it is a natural basshold as you have all the bait going in and coming out of the Channel. Would this area be worth fishing? Sure why not fish it and keep it honest. It is on the way to Coast Guard Channel, so do it up!

COAST GUARD CHANNEL

The US Coast Guard Station sits just inside this half mile long channel that dumps into Great Salt Pond. The pond is a huge nursery for every kind of baitfish that lives in the region, as well as clam farms. Quite often when I am up on Block I get my clamming license and go and rake clams for the grill. The things you learn by having fun! One day while I was raking the sand, sediment would stir off the bottom and in the "smoke" of the rake would be hundreds of sandeels balling up behind the rake and going crazy. I guess they were feeding on the worms or crustaceans I was stirring up as I raked. That same day as I raked, 50 yards from me I heard this commotion in the water and I looked over and I saw a bass of about 18 pounds blowing up on bait. It made me want to run up to the truck and grab my rod and a small popper.

So when the tide drops out of Great Pond you can probably imagine how good the fishing can be when the bass stack up. The Channel is not a regular spot for me on Block but there have been times when the weather and winds were foul that I had no other option but to fish it and it produced nicely as expected. One of my buddies that does a lot more eeling than I do has done very nicely there slinging eels out and opening the bail and letting the eel carry itself out with the tide.

I personally like to jig the channel in typical form, bucktails or rubber/leadhead combo's. I find the correct weight for the bottom and then I work my way down toward the area where the channel opens up, trying to find areas where the fish may be holding. Another good way to fish this area is by swimming hard plastics, or smaller bucktails along the edge of the channel and reeling them very slowly against the current. The channel is very close so you must be careful, there is no need to wade here. At night simply use your light to check for your drop off. Stay well away from the edge! Depending on the time of the year things can be good in the channel and it may be worth the effort. I do know that you have a shot at big bass in here too. With all the bait that dumps out of the pond it has to hold big bass. All summer while fishing on Block I always take a couple of nights to go down to the docks at Champlin's and jig for squid under the dock lights. The fact that there are squid means big baits and that means big bait enters the pond via the Coast Guard Channel—big bait, big bass.

THE DUMP

If you drive up Corn Neck Road you will come to West Beach Road on your left, which is the road that leads to the town's solid waste facility, or in layman's terms, the town dump. If you drive all the way to the end of the road you come to water, a place commonly referred to as "The Dump," at least that's the name I was taught.

This area is a long run in each direction consisting mostly of sand with a couple of slight rock promontories. The water here is relatively shallow so you will want some shallow-water swimmers to probe the area for bass. It honestly isn't a place I would normally fish unless I had good reason to.

One of the reasons I park here is to get to the north jetty of the Coast Guard Channel. The only way to access the north jetty is to park here and walk. I wanted to fish there because I thought it may be good on the incoming tide, so I hoofed it up there and I fished as I walked. I picked fish the entire way and picked up a couple on the back side of the channel, but it wasn't anything crazy good. What I did realize was that there were large amounts of spearing holding up near the jetty and I realized that whenever the wind blew hard northwest, the place would probably light up. I wrote that down in my journal for future use.

If you walked right from the Dump you would end up back up at Sandy Point, which is where we started.

WADERS ON BLOCK ISLAND

I have written here about fishing around Block Island, where most of my fishing is done in a wetsuit, but I want to emphasize that Block is extremely friendly to the wader-wearer, and the majority of the places I mention here are wader-friendly. Where the wetsuit guys usually fish the points and push out to the leading rocks, the wader fisherman can stay busy walking and working the edges of the points and the deep-water coves with no problem. I had a greenhorn with me one night at Dorry's and he worked the cove while the others went out and hit some outlying rocks. Well it wasn't long before he had a nice 28-pound bass on the sand and the look on his face that night will never leave me, it was like it was last night. It's an island in the Atlantic, go do your homework (scout) and go fish hard! Let the Block unveil itself to you!

CHAPTER FOUR

History of Block Island

Long before the explorers and Colonists came to America, Native Americans lived on Block Island, some believing they had lived on the island since 500 B.C.; others say some archeological evidence puts them there 30,000 years ago.

In any case, the Native Americans lived on the lands for thousands of years, happy, healthy and productive. They depended on corn (maize), hunting, shellfishing and fishing to sustain themselves. They were a peaceful people that worked hard and utilized all their resources. It is speculated that they were relatively non-violent because they were on the island and the only time they battled was when threatened by invasion.

The Native Americans on Block Island were known as the Manisses, the same as the island's original name, meaning, "Little God" or the "Little God's Island." The Manisses belonged to the Narragansett tribe. The Narragansett tribe had territorial divisions, each having a chief who was subject to the authority of a sachem or head chief. Ninicraft was the Narragansett chief of the Manisseans. The Narragansetts over on the mainland were more warlike, yet they understood the power of the English and sided with them militarily, especially against their arch-rivals the Mohegans and Pequots.

The influx of explorers, traders, and colonists brought trouble for the Native Americans. The Europeans brought sickness that they could not fight. They took the land they wanted, and they manipulated the Native Americans often causing tribes to fight each other more frequntly than they would have normally done, spurred on by promises of goods or money or "protection," and possibly the promise of weaponry.

The first recorded mention of Block Island came when an Italian, Giovanni da Verrazano, reported to Francis I of France in 1524, "It was full of hills, covered with trees, well-peopled, for we saw fires all along the coast." He named it "Claudia" in honor of Claude, the Duchess of Brittany, wife of Francis I. A few maps of the time also stated the name as "Luisa" after Louise of Savoy, the Queen Mother of France and mother of Francis I.

The first prominent event mentioned about Block Island was the Mohegan Bluffs incident, which took place in 1590. The Mohegans had invaded Block Island in order to capture it. When the Mohegans invaded, the Manisseans led them into a trap and eventually drove them off the 150-foot high bluffs, where they left them there to die without food or water. The Mohegan Bluffs area today, along the island's southern shore, is one of the most popular views on Block.

In 1614 Block Island was "discovered" by Dutchman Adriaen Block, who sailed from Manhattan Island (before it was bought from the Lenape tribe in 1626 by the Dutch), through Long Island Sound and eventually to Block Island, naming the island after himself. It was called "Adrian's

Adriaen Block laid claim to Block Island in 1614. He found it while sailing back to Holland from Manhattan Island upon his new ship the *Onrust*. Block was believed to be the first European to set foot on the island. (*Photo by dashinvaine*)

Eyland" on navigational maps for years until around 1664 when New Shoreham received its charter from Rhode Island, when it officially became Block Island. He is believed to be the first European to set foot on the island.

The Native American presence on Block Island began its decline with the arrival of John Oldham, a Puritan settler originally from the Plymouth Colony. He went on to do extensive trading with the Indians from Maine to New Amsterdam (New York). He did well trading between the Colonists and the Indians and he ended up back working for the Massachusetts Bay Colony.

In July of 1636 Oldham was at Block Island trading with the Indians, in all likelihood the Narragansetts. The Indians, one specifically, Audsah, ended up killing Oldham and his crew, his two nephews were captured, and the ship's cargo was looted. The nephews were later rescued and Audsah took off on the run. The Governor of Massachusetts ordered retaliation. The Bay Colony sent John Endicott to Block. He took 90 soldiers to kill all the braves they could find, burn the wigwams and canoes, and their vast stores of corn on the island's north neck. The John Oldham incident was the beginning of the end of the Native Americans on Block Island.

In 1661 the island was sold to sixteen settlers from the Massachusetts Bay Colony, who were seeking a democratic settlement free from religious persecution. The place they landed is called Settler's Rock marked today by a large rock monument. You can see it by driving to the top of Corn Neck Road—the monument is in the parking lot at the base of Cow Cove. The Native Americans on Block did not become hostile to the settlers because they feared the power of the English.

The numbers of the Native Americans on Block in 1662 was around 1,000. In 1700 they numbered 300 and by 1774 there were only 51 left. Their diminishing numbers were attributed to loss of land, many made into slaves, and

In 1636 a few of the Block Island Indians killed trader John Oldham and his crew. In retaliation the governor of Massachusetts sent John Endicott and 90 soldiers to punish them. They were waiting.

many left the island to fight on the mainland for their chief Ninicraft. There were no Indians killed on Block after the Endicott expedition.

From 1775–1783, during the Revolutionary War, the Block Islanders kept a lookout on Beacon Hill, lighting fires to warn that the enemy was in sight. In the 1800s, an observatory was built as a tourist attraction on Beacon Hill, the Island's highest point at 211 feet above sea level. The observatory is now a private home.

In 1829, the federal government built the Island's first lighthouse on Sandy Point. Sandy Point was a common spot for shipwrecks. Four lighthouses have since been built at this location. The present lighthouse, North Light, was built in 1867 and is sometimes open to the public for tours.

In 1854, the Spring House Hotel was built. It is the oldest hotel on the Island and still stands to this day, open to the public. Nicholas Ball built the Oceanview Hotel, the largest hotel on Block Island, in 1872. He made his fortune in the California Gold Rush of the 1840s. President Ulysses S. Grant stayed at the Oceanview Hotel and held a special session with the U.S. Supreme Court so its members would not have to interrupt their vacations by returning to Washington. The Oceanview Hotel burned to the ground in 1966.

"A majority of the inhabitants are farmers, not fishermen." (from *The History of Block Island*, Henry T. Beckwich 1857)

The federal government began building the breakwater in Old Harbor in 1870. It was completed in 1873, built mostly by islanders. Up to this point the island was inhabited primarily by farmers and fishermen. There were many on the island

The people of Block Island relied on farming and fishing as a way of life. Here men haul their pound nets. (*Photo courtesy of the Block Island Historical Society*)

that had never been to the mainland at all, the island was all that they knew. The breakwater at Old Harbor allowed for the steamships to come to the island, bringing a lot more people and tourists, and Block Island changed forever. The economy slowly changed from farming and fishing to tourism and summer homes.

In 1873, the Southeast Light was built on the cliffs 150 feet above sea level. It cost $75,000. In 1993, the Southeast Light was moved back 200 feet to escape the eroding bluffs. At the time it was the largest building ever to be moved in one piece.

In 1896, the Women's Christian Temperance Union erected the statue: "Rebecca at the Well," which stands in the center of town. Statues such as this were put in towns to supply water to horses, oxen, and dogs and also for men so they wouldn't have an excuse to go into a saloon to quench their thirst.

The Block Island State Airport was open and ready for use in 1950. Before this time, airplanes landed in the Sheep Meadow and in the minister's lot on Corn Neck Road. On a much more important note, the Airport Diner serves an excellent breakfast, especially for hungry surfcasters.

In 1971, the Block Island Conservancy was formed to preserve open space. Rodman's Hollow, a depression left by the glaciers, was one of the first sites to be preserved. Today about 44% of the island is preserved open space.

And I would be doing you a disservice if I didn't mention the legendary Captain Kidd was known to frequent Block Island prior to his being hanged for piracy.

SHIPWRECKS

Numerous shipwrecks have occurred off Block Island through the years, with at least five major wrecks. In 1738 the *Palantine* caught fire and went down off Sandy Point. In 1831 the two-masted schooner *Warrior* was wrecked, also off Sandy Point. In 1846 a ship carrying hard coal went aground in Cow Cove and this coal eventually replaced peat as the Island's major fuel source. In 1907 the steamer *Larchmont* collided with a three-masted schooner, the *Harry Knowlton*. Island fishermen were awarded gold medals from the Carnegie Foundation for their efforts in saving the survivors. Finally, in 1939 a 416-foot Texaco tanker, the *Lightburne*, went aground in front of the Southeast Lighthouse carrying 72,000 barrels of kerosene and gasoline. The crew was rescued and the ship was dynamited to create less of a navigational hazard.

THE 80s—GLORY DAYS OF BLOCK

Where Cuttyhunk has a rich history of fishing in the days of old that contribute to its legendary status, Block Island's surf fishing history came much later. The notable 1980s chiseled Block Island into the tablets of surfcasting history.

If you spend some time digging through Dennis Zambrotta's excellent account, *Surfcasting Around the Block*, it will not take you long to understand and visualize the world-class fishery that took place there in the 80s. For a couple of years and for reasons unknown, gigantic bass took up residence there, and there was a very good possibility that if you put in your time, you had a legitimate chance at a real trophy striped bass. Numerous 50- and 60-pound stripers were caught by surfcasters there.

Another good book written about adventures on Block Island was Leo Orsi's *Striper Chronicles*. Both books offer some very worthwhile reading!

CHAPTER FIVE

Cuttyhunk Island:
Introduction and Overview

Cuttyhunk Island is one of the most beautiful and remote places to fish for striped bass in the world. It is located in Massachusetts and lies within the town of Gosnold. It sits as the last island of the Elizabeth chain of islands. It was originally named Poocuohhunkunnah, by the Wampanoag tribe of Native Americans, which meant "land's end," or "point of departure." The name is almost longer than the island! On a clear day looking south and east across Vineyard Sound you can see the cliffs of Aquinnah on Martha's Vineyard. From the west side, if you look north and slightly west across Buzzards Bay you are looking at Westport, Massachusetts or Sakonnet, Rhode Island if you look a little further left. As the crow flies it is six and half miles to either the Massachusetts mainland or to Martha's Vineyard at its closest point.

You can only get to the island by boat. The ferry that you will take leaves from New Bedford and the ride is roughly 16 miles dock to dock and takes about an hour. For ferries you have two options, the *Cuttyhunk* M/V or The Cuttyhunk Water Taxi, *The Seahorse*—both are viable means for getting to and from the island.

Cuttyhunk has a very small village nestled into the east end of the island. The west end is vast and desolate. The island, as of this writing, has 11 adults and two kids who live on the island year-round, although by summer the population swells to about 500. The island itself is approximately ¾ of a mile wide and 2½ miles in length. You cannot take your vehicle to the island—once there you have to leg it to where you want to go or you can rent a golf cart. The islanders have golf carts, ATV's, or occasionally larger vehicles to get them around. The village itself has The Corner Store for gifts. The Island Market is a small market that carries essentials, and the Fish Dock, which in the summer months has a raw bar, ice cream shop, and lobsters for sale, has a good selection. But may I strongly suggest you bring everything that you think will need with you, especially in non-summer months, and I do mean everything. There are no tackle shops whatsoever on Cuttyhunk.

The Cuttyhunk Fishing Club was an integral part of the island from 1864 to 1922. The Club did a lot for the island, as it used folks from the community to work there. The Club donated the land for the first church on Cuttyhunk and helped erect the Gosnold Memorial on the West End in 1902.

When I go to Cuttyhunk I always stay at the Cuttyhunk Fishing Club Bed and Breakfast. I do so to support the Club and its place in surfcasting history. Please let me be clear, I have no qualms about any other accommodations, there are many very nice places to stay and relax. I just enjoy the Club mostly because of its rich history in striped bass fishing. The Club is basically the same as it was when it was still active, from 1865–1922. You can eat in the dining room where three sitting presidents did, and other great men who helped shape the country hung out when not fishing for striped bass. There is this really cool feeling you get when you are there, with old pictures on the wall all telling stories of yesteryear. These people from another time had the same passion as a lot of us do today. Somehow you end up feeling connected to it all. One of my favorite places to be in the entire world is on the edge of the bluff in front of the Club, sitting in an Adirondack chair and looking out over Vineyard Sound This is heaven to me. It is my center.

Once you settle in at the club it will not be long before you meet Bonnie Veeder, the caretaker of the Club. The Bass Queen, the Mayor of Cuttyhunk I call her. You will in all like-lihood hear her coming in a string of wisecracks and laughter, long before you see her. She is always smiling and happy and never shy of busting you down a couple of levels with a few quick remarks. If there is something you need to know about Cuttyhunk, Bonnie is your person. She is sixth generation on Cuttyhunk.

One of the first times I went to Cuttyhunk, I believe it was May, I just figured I could get food whenever I wanted like anyplace else. I got there with no food on Sunday and went hungry. Monday I went to the market for some groceries, but not only did I find out the store was only open one hour a day, but I also found a handwritten note that said, "off island until Thursday." Huh?! I survived thanks to Bonnie and a weekend wedding party that had just left, leaving behind plenty of left-over cold cuts and a case of beer. "It's all yours Darling!" I can still hear those beautiful words of Bonnie's today!

In the summer I highly recommend having breakfast out on the porch of the Club. It is a great place overlooking the Vineyard Sound and the bluffs of the Vineyard. There really isn't anything much better than a big breakfast after a long night of fishing on the rocks.

There are several other places where you can stay on Cuttyhunk. One of the most popular places is Pete's Place Rentals. They have several places you can stay. You can contact Lexi Lynch, who has been managing the places for some time now. You could also consider the Avalon, the Inn on Cuttyhunk Island, a big, beautiful place that overlooks the Club and Vineyard Sound.

The entire coastline of Cuttyhunk is rocks, boulders, and cobbles with the very small exception of Churches Beach and Barges Beach. Both provide a small area of sand for the beach chair. One of my favorite places to hang in the warm months is Channel Beach. You can watch the boats come in and out, lots of people swimming and enjoying summer. Bringing a light-action fishing rod with some Gulps isn't a bad idea either. See if there are any fluke or porgies at home.

TWO WAYS TO FISH

Stationary Fishing

When you fish Cuttyhunk, most of the time you will not have the ability to just up and move quickly to another place. Without easy transportation you usually tend to stay at a place longer, so I want to mention these two fishing techniques for Cuttyhunk. One is a stationary effort where you find a great spot and you stay there for a while and fish. This is the way I normally fish it. I spend a large amount of time in the daylight hours scouting and searching for my great spot. Top priority of course begins with a good comfortable rock, a boulder that has relatively easy access and one that I can stay on for hours. My next two major criteria are deep water and fast-moving water in front of my rock. I hunt tirelessly until I find my spot, never one that is simply adequate, but rather one that I absolutely love. I tell guys to find a spot that you "love," one that begs you to come and fish. I want to mention also that I am searching for a spot where I think fish (preferably big fish) will come to hunt, passing by me on a fish "highway." Such a spot is of course deep and with decent water movement, but very importantly, has to have a clear path to the open ocean, a place where big fish can easily move in from the depths. Once I find this spot I plan my night tides around fishing it. I like to scout by day the same tidal stage that I will fish at night. This way I can see seams, and get an idea of water speed. I look for submerged structure, things that I wouldn't normally or easily see under the cover of darkness. I also will figure out my best path of access to get to my boulder. I study the spot. If I get motivated sometimes I will even fish it by day to get a good feel for it. It is very important to swim your plugs in the water you will be fishing where you can see them swim, to learn the correct retrieve speed.

When the word Cuttyhunk is spoken it is usually accompanied by words like, "world class," "legendary," and "magical." Pulling big bass from the surf is the dream that draws most people to fish its waters.

After I identify a spot I plan on how I will attack it, what the best lures would be, perhaps the best weights for my bucktails or leadheads. Preparation is vital. I then return after dark or at dark and get my spot and begin fishing. I will stay on this rock for hours, a four-hour session would not be unusual. My entire premise here is waiting for fish, hopefully a big fish, to come by me. When I am prepared well I fish a spot like this with great confidence.

One night I went out to one of my carefully chosen rocks and began fishing. It was a rock that I had done well on consistently and was a spot I trusted. I had taken a 50 and several 40-pound bass from this spot. I had nothing for the first two and a half hours, which was very strange. When I went out to the rock I remember thinking how unusually warm the water was. I sat down on the rock to take a little break and to stretch my back a bit. I stuck my hand in the water and noticed it was a lot cooler than when I first went out, which made sense because the tide was coming in, bringing in cooler ocean water. That little observation gave me new hope. I got up and began fishing again, and fifteen minutes later I got a hit, a nice 20-pound fish. I followed that with eight fish in a row, all 20-pound class fish. I finished the session a couple of hours later with 17 fish, and a good night on the water. That is trust!

Moving to Fish

The second way to fish the island is by moving as you fish. When you are stationary you wait for fish to come to you, when you move you are now hunting for bodies of fish. Every once in a while I enjoy walking the rocky shoreline and just casting, either metal-lip swimmers or pencil poppers during the day. This is a much more relaxed mode and can easily be done with waders, you don't really have to go in the water. It's boulderfield fishing at its absolute best! Walk and cast, walk and cast. It is all sight casting, looking for structure and working a plug over top of it or beside it, places where bass hunt by ambush. There is nothing better than watching a metal-lip come swimming around a big boulder only to see that push of water behind it and the tail slap of a big bass in an explosion of salty brine. Working lures down the edge of the points into the coves is also productive as long as there is deep water. I usually do these sessions anytime in daylight hours, preferably overcast days with maybe some drizzle. A stiff wind creating whitewater is a bonus.

MY FISHING ON CUTTYHUNK

There are times when I and my fishing buddies can't get enough fishing at night so we sometimes will get the wetsuits on and do some daylight fishing in the boulderfields. Sometimes you can see some amazing stuff when the lights are on. My buddy Mark Jolliffe told a story about when he and another crony, Bill Lellis, were out doing some day work. Bill was working a pencil in and as it came up behind a huge boulder with some water cresting over it, Mark saw a monster bass pushing water behind Bill's pencil. Bill slowed the pencil as it came to the rock and Mark yelled to him to keep it going. Bill dragged the pencil across the top of the boulder and the bass came right up almost completely out of the water, across the top of the rock, chasing the pencil. Mark couldn't believe his eyes, he said the fish was huge. Bill never hooked the fish. That is the kind of thing that can happen anytime on Cuttyhunk.

On another day Mark and I were fishing the twin rocks ("Punk Rock") at the Pyramids well after sun-up, just doing some overtime, not quite ready to head back to the Club. Mark was on the rock to my right and penciling in between three rocks that I always called "three in line" because of the way they line up. It is always a good place to fish. So anyway I'm doing my thing and Mark is doing his, I'm not watching what he is doing but suddenly out of the corner of my eye I see this massive eruption on the surface behind the middle boulder. I look over to Mark and he is bent over along with his rod and he is holding on for dear life while this huge bass is thrashing on the surface right behind the rock! The fish was huge—it had to be over 50 pounds. It came unbuttoned. Mark was crying when he got his lure back with the hooks straightened and I was yelling at him about why he pulled so hard or something about drag setting. We talked about it the entire walk back to get breakfast and as a matter of fact, is something we still talk about to this day, always surrounded by good laughs and "what if's."

One thing about the island, as Bonnie Veeder always says, you can go out anytime of the day and catch a big bass on Cuttyhunk. Bonnie has numerous stories to support her claim. The big girls don't just swim close to shore at night; daytime is always in play on Cuttyhunk.

I have had the very good fortune of fishing this island extensively. A few years back I fished it every other week for two months. I started on Father's Day weekend in June, then three more consecutive trips to the island on my preferred tide and moon phase. What that allowed me to do was to watch a fishery unfold before me. That particular year, 2014, there were sandeels all over the place. I noticed this immediately upon arrival because of the heavy birdplay, which isn't terribly common on Cuttyhunk. There were terns all over and they were working constantly and they always had small bass under them, you could go out and catch 20 bass in an hour if the fish were close enough. The sand eels were small at first, maybe one inch long, you could see them in the beaks of the terns. Two months later the sand eels were still there but a lot bigger by that time, almost four inches long. I watched the sandeels grow and I watched the little bass feeding on them for two months, which was unusual, since normally either the bass or the bait would move on, but not in this case.

The other interesting thing was the bigger fish arriving. In June it was dink city. By mid-July it was still dink city but on one of the moons a nice body of bigger bass showed up and made their presence felt around the island. On a side note, usually when big fish show up, it isn't just in one spot. The one thing that I did notice this particular summer was how rough the surf was and it stayed that way for a month, very uncommon. It was a very powerful surf, very violent, especially on the West End. There you could really see it and feel it if you went in the water. The waves came in with an X-pattern. The water was so unpredictable I never felt safe, never relaxed. I'm not sure if it was the violent surf or the sandeel population but the big fish seemed to hang around for a month and make it worthwhile and fun!

When there is no good way to get from one side of the island to the other, you find one. Many nights we rode the ox trails hunting down big stripers on rented or borrowed ATV's.

We talked about tides and water movement and moon phases earlier in the book but I want to mention another time when I went up on back-to-back moons. The first trip was on the downside of the new moon. Mark and I went out and secured our rocks right at dusk. The water looked terrific, with great sweep, and the hit was smoking hot. I had something like nine fish on my first ten casts, all good fish. I remember hearing Mark hooting and hollering above the sound of the surf. Crazy! Well the week went like that, just good solid fishing, a few 30s, decent-size fish, no monsters, very few dinks. So I went home at week's end and readied myself for the next round two weeks (a moon phase) later. Well the big moon moved the one body of fish out and a new one in. Surprisingly, that week we all had good numbers but no one caught a fish over 14 pounds until the last night when one of us got a 30-pound fish. I remembered one of the great Cuttyhunk boat captains, Jimmy Nunes of the *Rudy-J,* who fished the Sow and Pig's, one of the most famous striper-holds in the world, for 50 years, once telling me, "the bodies of fish move in and out all the time." He'd say there would be all 20-pound fish for a few days, then they would be gone and then a body of big fish would move in, hang around a few days then nothing for a few days, then they would move on. It makes a lot of sense when you think about it, because as I mentioned the moon tides move bodies of fish in and out.

I love this photo for numerous reasons but mainly because it captures the call of Cuttyhunk and everything that has to do with our fishing there. Here are Mark and me out on Punk Rock putting in some time. You can see the Pyramids on the beach behind us. (*Photo Kevin Blinkoff*)

CHAPTER SIX

Fishing Cuttyhunk Island

CANAPITSIT CHANNEL

The Canapitsit Channel runs between Cuttyhunk and Nashawena, the large island neighboring Cuttyhunk, and the second in the Elizabeth chain. It is approximately 300 yards across to the other side. Access to Nashawena is prohibited as the island is privately owned by the Forbes family, and is primarily used for grazing cattle which you see at times down by water or in the water, cooling off, or licking the salt off the rocks. The channel has never done anything for me although technically it should be dynamite. It is a great pinch point and you would think that it would equal Quicks or Robinson's Holes but it does not. It is only about seven feet deep and usually has a lot of eel grass in it, making it not worth the long walk out. You also have to wade out a good distance on the edge of the channel to even get to deep enough water to fish.

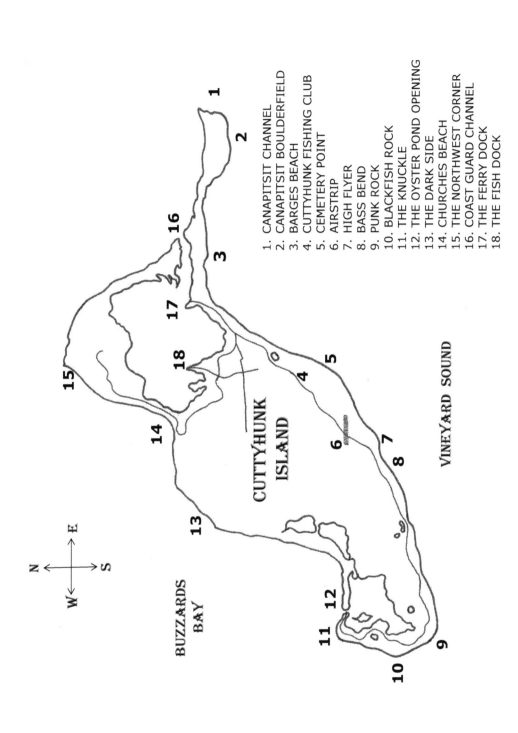

1. CANAPITSIT CHANNEL
2. CANAPITSIT BOULDERFIELD
3. BARGES BEACH
4. CUTTYHUNK FISHING CLUB
5. CEMETERY POINT
6. AIRSTRIP
7. HIGH FLYER
8. BASS BEND
9. PUNK ROCK
10. BLACKFISH ROCK
11. THE KNUCKLE
12. THE OYSTER POND OPENING
13. THE DARK SIDE
14. CHURCHES BEACH
15. THE NORTHWEST CORNER
16. COAST GUARD CHANNEL
17. THE FERRY DOCK
18. THE FISH DOCK

CUTTYHUNK ISLAND

VINEYARD SOUND

BUZZARDS BAY

N
E
S
W

Canapitsit Boulderfield

As you exit the channel to the south or towards Martha's Vineyard there sits a nice long boulderfield about 300 yards long. This has become one of my favorite places to fish because it holds fish and I usually do well in this area with pencil poppers in low light conditions. It gradually drops into deep water. On the Nashawena side there is a nice point that comes out parallel to the channel, which has a nice big rock on it that you can access from the rear. I call it the pulpit because you feel like you are standing in a pulpit. Once in position you have 180 degrees of water that you can work. This has been a spot where I just know I would hit a monster fish, yet I haven't, yet. I have caught a lot of fish but no really big ones.

The next spot is right in the middle of the field. There is a nice rock promontory that allows you to get out a decent distance and cast to some really nice looking water while you are looking out into open water with the Club off to your right in the distance. Fan your casts here and have some fun. Again the area holds fish and you should normally do well here with double digits.

At the other end of the boulderfield is another point, really a corner where you will need to push out. Mel Dorr's garage should be right behind you when you are in a good position. You have to get out far enough so you can cast into deep water, work towards doing that. There are a lot of shoaled out areas that you have to eliminate. I have seen some nice fish come out of this spot. One of the reasons it is productive is because, just off to your right, in the cove, there are a couple of huge eel-grass beds. Those beds hold small bait fish, and larger fish, like squid or hickory shad, come in to eat the smaller fish and then

From the top of Lookout Hill you can see the entire island. Here you see the old Coast Guard building and the channel into the harbor on the left. Barges Beach is in the middle and the Canapitsit boulderfield (upper right) just before Canapitsit Channel with Nashawena the next island beyond.

the bigger fish (stripers) come in and eat those fish. It is your ecosystem working for you and it is why the eel grass beds are so important. It is a good place for Super Strike Darters, providing decent distance and a good offering for big fish.

BARGES BEACH

Barges Beach was named after a series of 14 barges were put on that stretch of the neck in 1949 to act as a deterrent to erosion. The barges are more or less gone now so I call them the "skeletons" because that is all that is left. When you see them you will understand.

There is an "eel grass" bed just beyond the last barge up near the Canapitsit boulderfield which, when fished correctly, at the right tide, can produce nice fish, but you have to get into deep enough water adjacent to the eel-grass bed. The rest of the stretch is a long, gravelly, sandy beach leading back towards the Club which is relatively shallow with a sandy bottom. I have heard of some really good hits that have happened here with some good numbers of fish. It is a good wood needlefish stretch and very easy fishing.

I believe it was on my first trip to this beautiful island that, after being told in no uncertain terms that I would never see blitzing fish on Cuttyhunk, I had a major blitz of bass along this stretch where I caught ten or twelve bass in my first hour. I saw it as a welcoming from the Island Gods and I greatly appreciated it. I have not seen anything like it since.

UNDER THE CLUB

The next stretch of beach runs from two great tabletop rocks that sit at the bottom of the hill under the Club down just past the frog pond, to the area under the Club. The two tabletops have become recently exposed and have become very nice, easy-to-get-to platforms that allow you to cast to good water. I know of a nice bass caught there after Bonnie told some dude at the Club, watching TV, to get out and fish, and she told him where to go. He got up, went to the spot and pulled in a 38-pounder, making Bonnie once again the Queen of the Cuttyhunk bass!

The next and most notable spot under the Club is "the old bass stand." You can see the line of rocks clearly and you can see a few pipes left from when the Connecticut Surfcasters re-built a bass stand there in 1995. It was done to simulate the old bass stands, which we'll talk about in the next section of the book. I wish I could have been there to see it, and a big hat's off to those guys for doing that!

I have done very nicely on the leading rock of the line although its angle can make it a little uncomfortable to stay on for a long period of time. The one just behind it is much better for comfort. Out in front the water is nice and deep and there are both areas of sand as well as areas of rock and reef, and big fish often swim these areas while on lobster patrol. One night while throwing a Stetzko flaptail needle I hit a nice mid-20 on my second cast, then followed that up with a nice mid-30 on the next cast before busting the lure and fish off on the barnacle-encrusted rock, while trying to get a good photo of the fish. To the right of the bass stand there are a couple of nice perches in the next 100 yards, for a surfcaster wanting to flirt with a big girl. This area, especially the bass stand, is also a great eeling spot.

CEMETERY POINT

If you go just a bit further you will come to a beautiful bouldery point that we nicknamed, "Cemetery Point." We called it that because of a shortcut we take through the cemetery that drops us right on that point. This point is the first of several awesome points that run down that side of the island. Out on the leading edge of this extended point you can find a couple of nice rocks to fish from. Once you get past this point you drop into a long cove. If you walk this area and cast to boulders or submerged structure you can pick fish all along. What we sometimes do is to go out on overcast or rainy days and walk and cast. The fishing includes a lot of pencil popper action, watching bass blow up on your offering with the lights on is sweet, there is very little better than that! I also throw a lot of metal-lip swimmers in these coves and occasionally will tie into a heavyweight.

At the end of this long cove you will find another point—you are now getting into some great bass water. This point also produces (as all will). Then there is a smaller, deep-water cove and then another point. This cove has a big tabletop boulder in it that you have to swim to, if you're experienced in wetsuiting and swimming onto rocks. (Yet again, *don't try this without prior practice*.) It is a great platform once you get on it and this cove will produce the biggest bass. This is good eeling area as your chances of a lulu loom large! I also like throwing my big leadhead/rubber combo's here. The other point of this small cove is another very good point to push out onto and get access to some great water straight out as well as back into the cove to your left, but from a different angle.

HIGH FLYER

If you walk the road out from town, you will pass over the air strip, walk a bit and then come to a sharp incline. Go up and over the hill and down the other side, and at the bottom there will be a path on your left that leads to the edge of the bluff. You will be looking out into the water, the point below you is the last one I talked about in the section above. This trail we started calling the "High Flyer" years ago because someone threw a High Flyer in the brush up by the road so it was our landmark. (A high flyer is a reflective marker attached to a long pole and float, used by commercial fishermen to mark where their nets begin and end.) This trail is the only trail on this side of the island giving you access down to the water. Down the bluff and off to the right is a sprawling point with great looking water. Off the beach a ways is a huge boulder

Cuttyhunk's entire south side is boulderfields such as this. Points and coves providing ambush points and hunting grounds for striped bass. Walking and casting in these areas can produce some nice fish on metal-lip swimmers and poppers.

that the Long Island guys call the "School Bus." It's the size of a school bus, although we used to call it the "Wooly Mammoth" because that is what it looked like to me. For those that don't mind a swim it is a great bass platform. This entire area is fishy and I have caught fish all along here.

BASS BEND

When you walk passed the oversized point you will come to your next cove, called "Bass Bend." It's a good name and I don't know where it came from but it fits, because the bass in this slot will bend your hooks straight. Ask Don Guimelli from Afterhours Custom Plugs, he loves this cove. He has had lures destroyed here by big fish. This is an absolutely a great spot.

BASS BEND TO PYRAMIDS

The next stretch from Bass Bend down to the Pyramids is a good stretch of boulders but is seldom fished due to lack of access. The quickest way to get here would be by going to the West End, walking left and then keep walking for fifteen minutes. It would be a good fifteen minutes from High Flyer coming from the other direction as well. It's a good area if you want to get away from people. This area seems to change quite a bit from year to year but is productive. The key of course would to be sure to find deep water in front of you and then I would love your chances!

THE WEST END

The West End has a couple of names, "Southwest Point," and "The Pyramids" are the most common ones you will hear. You can get there by walking west from town. Once the paved road ends it is about a 20 to 25-minute walk. The west end is desolate. This area is a commonly fished area as it is the beginning the famous reef known as the "Sow and Pig's," a place of legend among striper fishermen, more to boat fishermen than to surfcasters. It has also taken its fair number of ships through the years, a graveyard for ships that could not navigate this treacherous reef that extends out about a mile from land's end.

As you walk down the main (former ox) trail, you will know it when you are getting to the end as the trail will open up to water in front of you. This is the West End, also known as "heaven" to the striperman. Roughly about 70 yards before you get to the big opening, where the trail makes a hard right,

The West End is also called "the Pyramids," four concrete bases to a radar tower that once stood high upon the bluff during wartime. The West End is where the famous Sow and Pig's Reef starts and extends out for a mile.

you will find a small path that leads down to the water. If you walk down and go to your left a short ways you will see where the term "pyramids" comes from. There are four concrete pyramids that were once the base of a radar tower in World War II. The bluff they were on eroded and down they came. I don't think they will be going anywhere anytime soon. Now if you go past the pyramids you will come to a long boulderfield that has potential. I have had some good fish here but you have to push out and get a good platform. This area changes quite a bit from year to year as does the entire West End. Sometimes it shoals out and sometimes it is nice and deep. Either way it is worth the effort.

Right on the corner at the Pyramids, out about 30 yards, you will see two big flat rocks right beside each other. I have always loved this spot. We have called it "Punk Rock" for over ten years because one time we were there and there was this kid in a wetsuit fishing on it, and someone asked, "Who's that punk on our rock?" Hence the name was born. The water here sweeps beautifully around this area and bass are usually not far away. It can be a little shoaled out at times from one year to the next in front, but the bass love the fast water. Darters, bucktails, leadheads, and of course pencils are great here. This area also gives you more than 180 degrees to cast between the two rocks, because you can jump from one to the other.

BLACKFISH ROCK

On the West End there is a huge rock that sits right in the middle of the west-facing side and if you look closely at it you will see the remains of an old bass stand. This we call Blackfish Rock and it is hard to miss. It got its name because Bill Lellis either fished off of it or right beside it and one night he hooked two nice fish that swam underneath him and sawed him off. So the next day Bill got his snorkeling stuff and went and did some investigating. He found that the underside of the rock was all scoured out and formed a ledge. As he dove the area he found a 60-yard-long trough that was loaded with blackfish, hence the name Blackfish Rock came to be. I have caught some very nice bass from this area, you can see why.

Now the area between Punk Rock and Blackfish Rock is a long bouldery run that has some nice wetsuit rocks that sit out a bit. This area gets some nice sweep and can produce nicely for you. It is a great pencil spot and it is a very nice 2-ounce wood needle spot, I've done great here with Hab's 2-ounce needle. The wind comes into play here too as does some surf. Rough is good! I said this is a good wetsuit spot but it can also be done in waders, providing the water is deep enough. You wade out as far as you safely can and cast into the sweep and let the lure work for you. The ability to throw a long cast will help tremendously.

When you walk past Blackfish, you have roughly a 200-yard field. This area is rarely fished for some reason but it can be worth an extra five- or ten-minute walk away from the Pyramids. This is prime water, blackfish and lobster abound. I've taken some nice fish out of this area. I recall one night I turned my light on and I saw a nice school of squid swimming right out in front of me, not a bad sign at all.

THE KNUCKLE AND OYSTER POND OPENING

The very north end of the west end is what I have nicknamed "The Knuckle" because at times it seemed to stick out like the knuckles of a fist. The water sweeps past the Knuckle very nicely here. I am intrigued by this spot and have fished it on the logic that if there are big fish on the reef, they should pass this point when heading east into Buzzards Bay. It is usually a schoolie spot, although one night I did pull a 25-pounder out of here so big fish must move through here. For me it is also a play spot and I do a lot of experimentation because of the numbers of fish available. If you wade out and fish, throwing rigged Slug-Go's, 1-once bucktail, or SP Minnows, you should have no trouble pulling double digits for the night once you find the slot where the fish are set up.

WASH POND COVE

This cove is a long shallow cove that connects the "Knuckle" to another boulderfield on the other end, probably a stretch of about 400 yards. The notable thing about this cove is that it has the Oyster Pond opening. Anywhere you go in the world to fish, wherever you have any kind of a pond or lake that dumps into a bigger body of water, you naturally have a great place to fish. Anyplace where fry or juvenile fish can seek safe harbor and grow and then at some point leave the pond you have great fishing potential, and this place is no different. There are really three ponds back here, two saltwater-fed ponds and a freshwater pond that connects them. The amount of fry in these three ponds can be unbelievable. I have walked these ponds at night and have lit up the water with my light, the amount of spearing in both ponds was the most I have ever seen anywhere. I would love to be around that area when the bait dumps out of those ponds!

This cove is big and relatively shallow. If you work you can find a couple of its deeper spots and you could have multiple-fish nights—and I mean 30–50 fish when they are on the feed. You would be hard pressed to get a keeper, however. When you have water that is that shallow you want to hit this area on higher tides, as the pond is flushing on the outgoing tide. Shallow-water swimmers, Slug-go's, and small wood needles shine here.

This area is the furthest area from town, out near the Gosnold Memorial. Walking from the Pyramid it is another 20-minute walk on the same trail, or you could walk the shoreline, but that is a tough go as well. It's a hump. It will however take you past the old lighthouse ruins where you will see where the Cuttyhunk Light once stood.

BACKSIDE

As we move further along, as you leave the cove you will come to a place where suddenly a new boulderfield begins. This is the roughest terrain on the island and it is the furthest and hardest to get to. The next half mile of shoreline, from there to Churches Beach, is the area I call the "darkside of the moon" as few venture back here. I never fished this stretch for the first few years I fished Cuttyhunk. The water here is good. It is very deep. If you go out 15 feet, the water will be over your head. It drops right off. It also pulls nicely on this side (as it does on both sides). If you venture back here throw rubber/leadheads, bucktails, and eels.

The backside of Cuttyhunk is another long boulderfield with a beach notched out of it called Churches. This area offers deep water with less surf accompanied with good moving water and unforgettable sunsets. (*Photo Matt Risser*)

CHURCHES BEACH

I call the entire "U-shaped" cove Churches. If you are standing on the beach at Churches looking straight out, which would actually be northwest, there is a nice area of rocks out to your left. Anywhere along this edge fish can be caught. I have seen any and all lures produce here. If you get out to that far left point, there are a couple of nice rocks there, but you will have to wetsuit to them. Once you get one you will have a great perch for the night! When I fish here I cast almost straight north. You will see the silhouette of Penikese Island, cast towards that and retrieve back slow, in the fast-pulling current and you could end up with a nice double-digit night and always a shot at a lulu. Lean heavily on your bucktails, rubbers, and darters here.

If you go to the right of Churches Beach you have another boulderfield that you will pick up where the sand turns to rocks. This is another stretch of rough terrain to walk on. You will find fish all along this stretch although you may have to work to find a pocket of fish or a flat rock. This is another area where you won't find many guys because it is remote and out of the way of everything. A good friend of mine, Mark Garahan, had a great night in this stretch where he landed over 50 bass and I remember it was on a Beachmaster Junior. Why do I remember that? Because I remember my shock when he told me that he hung the lure up in a lobster pot rope and he was so afraid of losing this "hot" lure that he stuck his rod in the rocks and dove in and followed his line down to the rope where he proceeded to cut his prize lure free and get it back! Now that my friend is attachment!

"NORTHEAST CORNER"—COPICUT NECK

If you go roughly 200 yards across unfriendly boulders you get to what I call the "Northeast Corner." Here the island makes a hard right turn and you are now on a corner. On this corner is a nice flat, friendly rock, a spot that has been good to me over the years. If the water is pulling well you can cast straight west (watch out for the big boulder) and let the offering sweep north (assuming an incoming tide). Try to keep it deep. You can also cast again straight north, straight at Penikese. I have never hit any legit cows from this spot but I have had some good-number nights when the fish were there, with fish up to the high 20s. Big fish do come by this spot!

Now if you move to your right you will hit shallow water—no good.

THE CHANNEL

An outflow is a great place to fish, especially when the pinch point is fairly narrow, which it is coming out of Cuttyhunk Harbor. However I have not spent any serious periods of time fishing this stretch. I have fished it in passing numerous times but never put any serious planning or effort into the spot. Don't be angry with me—after all on Cuttyhunk there are bigger areas to attack, with "bigger" possibilities if you know what I mean!

There is a very nice spot out on the end of the neck where the channel seems to dump into the Canapitsit Channel. I have fished this spot, but with very little success so far, but I wouldn't be surprised if it produced.

We have concluded our circling of the island. Remember there is an endless list of potential good spots here and the secret ingredients to success will be scouting endlessly. Nothing beats good old fashioned hard work!

CHAPTER SEVEN

History of Cuttyhunk Island

Cuttyhunk Island is loaded with the intrigue and legend of surfcasting history. It has enough documented history to be credited as the birthplace of surfcasting in America. While it was not surfcasting in the way we do it today, it still consisted of a person on land trying to catch a fish from shore in a recreational setting. It almost certainly started here on Cuttyhunk Island, followed closely by the Pasque Island Club which opened a year later. It mystifies me as to why did it start in 1865. Why that year? How did a bunch of rich business men come up with that idea? If you think about it on a timeline of American history, the west was still wild in 1865. To give it perspective, Abraham Lincoln was assassinated five days after the Club was formed on April 9, and the United States only had 35 states at the time.

But let's back it up a bit. The island was originally named Poocuohhunkkunnah, it is speculated that it came from the Wampanoag name for "Point of departure" or "Land's end." In 1602 an English explorer, Bartholomew Gosnold, renamed the island Cuttyhunk, (apparently he had trouble with the Wampanoag pronunciation as well!).

Gosnold established a modest fort on Cuttyhunk, in the area where the Gosnold Memorial now stands. One of the original purposes of his voyage was to begin a colony in the New World. After exploring the islands for less than a month, the men returned to England on his barque *The Concord*. They took with them a load of sassafras trees, which had substantial value in Europe.

Two hundred and sixty three years later a fishing club was established on Cuttyhunk. In 1864 a group of wealthy men, mainly from Manhattan and Philadelphia, wanted to establish a place to go and fish. After a visit to Cuttyhunk they decided they had found their spot. They purchased a large portion of the island and began work. These men sought out a place primarily for fishing but also as a social platform to be used for political and social networking—after all these were powerful men from huge "Gentlemen's Club's" in New York

An artist rendering of the Cuttyhunk Fishing Club in it's heyday. (*Photo courtesy of the Cuttyhunk Historical Society*)

City and Philadelphia. These were influential men who helped forge and shape the country on many levels. A few among the ranks were John Archbold, President of Standard Oil; George and Pierre Lorillard, tobacco heirs and avid sportsmen; Howard McGown, who ran a steamship line in the Hudson River; Jay Gould, railroad tycoon; and William McCormack of International Harvester. The Pasque Island Club, two islands up the Elizabeth Islands chain, was founded right around the same time and it too had men of influence. Both clubs were very similar, with only one glaring difference, The Cuttyhunk Club did not allow women and children, while the Pasque club embraced them.

The Cuttyhunk Club limited initial membership to fifty men. New members had to be sponsored by an existing member and needed a majority vote by the executive board. A single negative vote from an active member was sufficient to bar a man from membership. The admission fee was $300. Dues were $100 per year, which covered much of the expenses of running the club. Often there would be an assessment to cover the club's budget shortfalls. There was also a charge for meals and the nightly stay at the Club. Records were kept of the alcohol consumption and payment was expected upon departure. Eventually, the membership was expanded to sixty, then seventy-five. The Club membership totaled over 270 men during its 60 years of operation.

Cuttyhunk was a prestigious club that also became known as the "President-Maker" because of the members who became President of the United States, including Chester A. Arthur, Theodore Roosevelt, and William Howard Taft. Grover Cleveland stayed there as a guest.

The old bass stands were bridges to the sea, allowing the angler to get out past the breakers into fishable water. The stands were wood platforms with steel supports anchored into boulders. Remnants of the old stands can still be seen today. (*Photo courtesy C.H.S.*)

While the Cuttyhunk and Pasque Island clubs developed there were also other clubs springing up all over the area: West Island, Squibnocket Club, Block Island Club, and Graves Point Fishing Club in Newport. There was even one on Noman's Land Island.

With the rise of the Cuttyhunk Club, the island developed and changed in many positive ways. The Club had a lot of expenditures, they had to pay the staff, buy supplies and keep the grounds. They built a clubhouse and a barn, an ice pond and two ice houses, and a superintendent's cottage. They built a dock and had to dredge the channel to make it deeper and wider. They grew all their own vegetables in the area between the club and where the road is now. The island was mostly barren and grass covered, without trees as Gosnold and the English had stripped the island clean of its trees. Several hundred sheep continually grazed the island grass, 300 of which were owned by the Club. Early on the Club also kept carrier pigeons that would carry messages back and forth to the cities as the new technologies, such as phone lines, were not yet in use on Cuttyhunk.

The Club did a lot for the island of Cuttyhunk beside provide jobs. They donated land for the first church, which still stands today. They had a hand in the erection of the Gosnold Memorial in 1902 where Bartholomew Gosnold had built his encampment back in 1602. The area consists of a small island named Gosnold Island located in the West End Pond, where The Memorial still stands today. The Club donated the stone and sand needed to build the monument. Club member Charles Randall helped raise $3,000 for the construction costs. (On a side note I understand that German U-boats were considering blasting the memorial during World War II because they thought that it may have been a radar tower for the Americans.)

The bass stand would have a "gentleman" who fished and a chummer, usually an islander who would, chum bait the hook, and gaff fish. The main baits of the day were menhaden and lobster. (*Photo courtesy C.H.S.*)

The club stayed open basically from May through September each year, during the good years, providing jobs for many of the islanders.

They fished utilizing bass stands, which were long wooden platforms supported by steel stanchions that stretched out from rock to rock into the surf. Such stands were all around the island. Each stand had a name, such as: Old Waterline Rock, Nashawena Point, Gull Rocks, Little Bass Rock, Big Bass Rock, Mussel Bed Rock, Sheep Pen Rock, and Cove Point. The stands allowed the men to get out into the surf and out into great bass water. In fishing around the island I have found the remains of at least 16 of the 26 bass stand rocks. You can see holes that were drilled in the rocks and on rare occasions you can find what is left of the steel stanchions. Having fished this island extensively, I can verify that the locations of the old bass stands are always in really good bass water! They definitely did their homework.

Each evening, the members of the Club would meet to draw lots to determine who got what stand the next day. Each member employed a "chummer," a person, usually always an islander, who took care of the gentleman in the tradition of ghillies in Scottish salmon fishing. Chumming was the main method used for catching these striped bass, with lobster and menhaden being the good cheap baits of the day. They would pay the chummer $1 per fish caught, or more if the fish were particularly large. Records were kept of the number, size, and location of the fish caught, and by whom. It was the responsibility of the chummer to be sure that the bass were correctly weighed and entered into the record. This was done in the presence of two members to avoid mistakes. Members fished in the pre-dawn hours, sometimes as early as 3 a.m., but were due back to the club for a large breakfast. Lunch was not served at the Club. Supper on the other hand was an extravagant event with numerous courses with very good food and plenty of drink. Notably each member had a liquor locker to store his alcohol in.

The fishing consisted of the member and chummer going out onto the end of one of the stands—the chummer would toss chum and the member would cast. Once a fish was hooked the chummer would help get the fish in and eventually gaff the fish and get it ashore. The rods and reels of the early Clubs were primitive—reels consisted of wood spools, with the drag being basically a small flap of leather that was pushed against the spool. I would have imagined this being very inconvenient and I am sure these old reels inflicted many nasty burns! Rods were made of bamboo and were seldom over eight feet long. There were numerous 50- and 60-pound fish caught at the early bass clubs and one can be fairly certain that many were unstoppable until the better reels showed up, which they did.

When a member caught a large bass he was awarded the prestigious "High Hook" award, which was a diamond-studded hook. The fisherman would wear it until a bigger fish was caught. The hook belonged to the Club and was worn only while on Cuttyhunk. A smaller diamond-studded hook was also awarded for the smallest fish caught. At the end of the season the angler with biggest bass was awarded the High Hook. The member with the first fish caught of the season wore both pins.

The cart is loaded and ready to go. The men drew for their stand. The horse and wagon dropped them off and picked them up at their spots. (*Photo courtesy C.H.S.*)

For many years the clubs thrived. The membership was robust and the stripers kept everyone smiling, the 1870s, 80s and early 90s were very good times. However by the late 1900s the bass population was beginning to dwindle badly. There was a lot of speculation at the time that the bass stocks were dropping because of the large amount of menhaden that were being harvested from Buzzards Bay. There was a lot of bad blood about all of the menhaden being taken out of Buzzards Bay and it was widely thought that the over-harvesting directly affected the bass stocks. Members of the Pasque Club were very active in trying to protect the waters, but the fight was useless.

High Hook Record

Pasque Island Club

Year	Date	Name	Strand	Weight
1866	June 26	Jacob L. Dodge		58 lb
1867	July, 26	William L. Barker		36 lb
1868	July, 6	Edw. Phalon		61 lb
1869	Sept. 2	A. B. Dunlap		62 lb
1870	July, 11	Peter Balen		30 lb
1871	Sept. 17	P. C. Harmon	6a	34 lb
1872	July, 30	Tho⁵ E. Tripler	4	44 lb
1873	Aug. 15	E. O. Herring	15	??
1874	Aug. 1	Tho⁵ E. Tripler	11	53 lb
1875	July, 2	Jo⁵ J. O'Donohue	11a	52 lb
1876	July, 3	Peter Balen	4	50 lb
1877	Sept. 19	A. F. Higgins	15	47 lb
1878	July, 28	E. O. Herring	1	60 lb
1879	Sept. 30	T. D. Barrett	1	51 lb
1880	Sept. 30	William Dunning	11	49 lb
1881	Aug. 3	W⁵ H. Phillips	4	27 lb
1882	Aug. 24	C. P. Cassilly	11	54 lb
1883	Sept. 19	A. B. Dunlap	12	23 lb
1884	Aug. 15	C. P. Cassilly	4	49 lb
1885	Sept. 28	A. F. Higgins	18	34 lb
1886	Aug. 14	W⁵ H. Phillips	4	25 lb
1887	July 6	J. L. Vallotton	4	32 lb
1888	Aug. 27	Hy. Stettinius	1	44 lb
1889	Aug. 10	S. Humphreys	4	16 lb
1890	Aug. 11	E. Delano	6	49 lb
1891	Sept. 19	John F. Scott	11	19½ lb
1892	July 27	A. W. Durkee	Q&H	26 lb
1893	July 26	John F. Scott	6½	58 lb
1894	Aug. 15	N. W. Meserole	6a	34½ lb
1895	July 30	Henry Stettinius	6	42 lb
1896	Aug. 4	W⁵ H. Phillips.	6	89½ lb
1897	Sept. 3	Cha⁵ D. Ladier.	16	27 lb
1898	Sept. 19	A. F. Higgins.	4	24 lb
1899	Sept. 4	A. F. Higgins.	4	58 lb
1900	July 10	Cha⁵ J. Carpenter	4	38 lb
1901	July 20	W⁵ H. Phillips	4	28 lb

Each year a "High Hook" was awarded. Careful records where kept of the catches. Here you can see the biggest fish caught from the Pasque Island club from 1866–1901. (*Photo courtesy C.H.S.*)

As the fish disappeared the clubs lost popularity and faded. The older members were dying off and their children had little interest in continuing on with the club. At Cuttyhunk in 1902 only two bass were recorded, in 1912 they were down to just one stand. Over at Pasque it was more of the same, 1902 showed only 40 fish taken, for the years 1910 and 1911 records read, "No bass taken." Then at Pasque it was two more years of bass, then from 1914–17 "No bass taken." Finally in the slots for 1918–19 it was written, "Club Closed during War." Pasque ceased operations in 1917.

I could not mention Cuttyhunk history without mentioning William Madison Wood, whose fingerprints are all over Cuttyhunk. He was a member of the club from 1904 until 1916. He loved Cuttyhunk and called it his paradise. In 1909 he purchased the land across the street from the club and built the Avalon, the huge beautiful house that sits across the street, up on the hill. He also built a bigger house up on top of the hill in 1917 called the Winter House. If you stay on Cuttyhunk for any length of time and end up doing some walking into or through town, you will soon learn of the walkways that Wood put in place to get across the island quickly, which still make very nice shortcuts to get to where you are going. You will also notice that there are no unsightly overhead power lines on Cuttyhunk—this too was Wood's doing, putting all the power lines underground as well as installing a new sewer system. He was a great thinker, much ahead of his time.

In the final season only three members visited the Club, and Wood bought the remaining holdings of the Club and closed its doors for good in 1922. It was the end of an era!

The Club was purchased by Mr. and Mrs. Robert Moore in 1948 and they lived there until it was bought back into the Wood family. All parties took great care of the Club and honored it. Much of it is the same today as it was in the days of yesteryear. Today it is the Cuttyhunk Fishing Club Bed and Breakfast, run by Bonnie Veeder. Anyone is welcome to stay there from Memorial Day to Columbus Day, and I would strongly recommend you doing it at least once!

Cuttyhunk Lighthouse

Cuttyhunk had a lighthouse that warned ships out on the Sow and Pig's reef on the West End. The lighthouse was in service from 1823–1947. It stood adjacent to the Gosnold Memorial. All that is left standing today are the remnants of the oil building which was built in 1903. If you go out that way you will still find the foundation of the house and some smaller remaining foundations. The Sow and Pig's took many ships upon her rocks.

This post card circa 1910 pictures an unidentified ship wreck and observers using a bass stand for a better view. It is believed this took place on the West End.

Index

About the Author

D. J. Muller is a well-traveled surf-caster who enjoys sharing his extensive experience and knowledge with others. *Surfcasting Block Island and Cuttyhunk* is DJ's fifth book on surfcasting—others are *The Surfcaster's Guide to the Striper Coast, Striper Strategies, Striper Tales,* and *Fishing the Cape Cod Canal.* He lives on Pelican Island, NJ. He can be reached at: djmull1313@gmail.com.